DREAMS

== *for your* ==

GRANDCHILD

DREAMS

for your

GRANDCHILD

The _Hidden Power_
of a Catholic Grandparent

ALLEN R. HUNT

WELLSPRING
North Palm Beach, Florida

Design by Ashley Wirfel

ISBN: 978-1-63582-002-7 (hardcover)
ISBN: 978-1-63582-015-7 (softcover)
ISBN: 978-1-63582-016-4 (ebook)

Library of Congress Control Number: 2018947140

10   9   8   7   6   5   4   3   2   1

Printed in the United States of America

DEDICATION

To Mimi,
World-Class Grandmother

———————————

My grandpa died tonight. He's the one who taught me what it means to be a man and how to be a Catholic man. We knew he probably didn't have long, but that doesn't make it any easier. Please pray for the repose of his soul and for my family. Thank you!

— Prayer request from a Dynamic Catholic Ambassador

PRAYER FOR GRANDPARENTS

Lord
We are privileged to know
The blessing of grandparents

To know
The knowledge of years
The wisdom of fears
The gift of tears

To know the warm embrace
The kindly face
The unjudging space
The listening place

Lord
May we follow
In footsteps
That honor the mystery of their giving
The sacrifices of their living
Their gracious forgiving

May they find in us
Warm compassion
And endless passion
For life and love
May we move to the gentle rhythm
   of their living
May we cherish them with empathy
   and patient giving

May we know the sacredness of faith
Blessed by their constant believing

In you, Lord
In life
In love
In trust
In truth

May they be free from
Anxiety
Pain and sorrow

May they find in each other
A faithful companion
Where silence is the bridge
To blessed memories of
Other times and other days
May they never be lonely
Because we are too busy
May our words of gratitude and
   thanks
Never be empty
May the fruits of their lives
Ripen into a harvest of plenty

May they find joy
In their children's children
In the company of loved ones
In the warm embrace of old friends
In the knowledge that your promise
Never ends

Lord bless them
All the days of their lives

(Fr. Liam Lawton, *Hope Prayer*)

CONTENTS

═══════

PROLOGUE: MY NEW NAME

You were not made for comfort.
You were made for greatness.
—Pope Benedict XVI

I stepped through the door of the newborn intensive care unit (NICU) with fear and trembling. Through security's double doors. Down the corridor. Into the unit filled with tiny newborn children. My eyes quickly noticed the small plastic cradles, each holding an infant born prematurely and needing all the medical attention he or she could get just to stay alive. This was a place of life and death.

When I found my daughter's newborn son, Allen Joseph, I froze. I just stood there. It was the first time I had ever seen him. And it was there in the hospital NICU. I'd never expected a moment like this.

Born prematurely and struggling to expand his little lungs to breathe, there lay my first grandchild. When I received the news he was entering the world about a month before he was due, I drove furiously from a speaking engagement half a continent away to get there as soon as I could. My wife, Anita, had battled every imaginable obstacle the day before to be with our daughter as she gave birth. And Anita had watched as they loaded little Allen into the ambulance to take him from his birth hospital to the NICU in a larger hospital ten miles away.

I stared at little Allen. His tiny body was swaddled in a blanket and connected to tubes and machines all around him. The nurse softly told me I could touch him but not to pick him up or jar him in any way. As I placed my index finger on his miniature cheek, tears streamed down my face. Welcome to the world, Allen Joseph.

That's when it happened. A new dimension of my heart opened, one I did not even know I had, one that allowed me to love in an entirely new way. It happened in an instant. I didn't ask for it. My heart just stretched and grew a whole new chamber. My first grandson. Little Allen. From the very first moment I saw him, I loved him. I loved every single ounce of him. And I knew I would never be the same. After all, life-changing events tend to be life-changing.

Each day, my daughter, my son-in-law, Anita, and I waited. Allen's premature birth and his still-forming lungs placed our hopes and dreams for this little child in jeopardy. Our family prayed. We waited, we sat near him when we were allowed into the unit, and we held him when the nurses permitted. Then we waited some more.

We watched as some premature babies were released and allowed to go home. We witnessed the challenges of other exhausted families whose newborns had been in the NICU for months, families who were still uncertain whether their child would survive. We prayed for each of them. And our family waited . . . and waited.

When Allen Joseph's vital numbers began to improve, we rejoiced as the doctors told us he could go home. After seven days of restricted access and excellent care in the NICU, he would be going home with his mom and dad.

That moment marked a new day for Anita, our family, and me. A new season of life, really.

When Anita and I dated, she called me Allen. Once we were engaged, she began to call me "sweetie." After our wedding, she called me "hubby." Soon after our first daughter was born, Anita referred to me as Daddy.

But now I have a new name: Grandpa. Since Allen's birth, my daughters have given birth to two more grandsons, and we are expecting a fourth even as I write this prologue.

We have hopes and dreams for each grandson: Allen, Sam, Matthew, and Michael. We even have dreams for the ones still to come. But our deepest desire is that they each will lead great lives. We want them to be happy. We pray each will find life in Jesus and His Church. To become the-best-version-of-themselves, our grandchildren will need all the help God can give them.

As much as I love little Allen, God loves him even more. God loves with an infinite, unconditional, generous love. And He made Allen for greatness, for happiness with Him.

God has great dreams for each child. After all, we are made for greatness. And He calls grandparents to help our grandchildren achieve it. God has given us this new vocation, the life of a grandparent. And we intend to make it count. I knew from the moment I met my first grandson that I was all in.

PART ONE:
WHAT'S AT STAKE

1. YOUR DREAMS

Choose this day whom you will serve ... but as for me and my house, we will serve the Lord.

—Joshua 24:15

I hear it every time.

Last year, I spoke in twenty-five states. In parishes, arenas, schools, funeral homes, business seminars, and fund-raising galas. And in almost every setting, the same question popped up.

The Number One Question I Get Asked

It usually happens like this.

An older man walks up alongside me and whispers, "Can I ask you something in private?" We find a room or a hallway and stand in a quiet place for just a moment.

I see the pain in his face and ask, "How may I help you?"

"I am worried about my grandchildren. They don't go to Mass. What can I do?"

"Tell me about your family," I say.

First, I see the pain. Then, I hear it.

"They are all just so busy. My kids work. My grandchildren play soccer, and spend lots of time on their computers and phones. They are all so busy doing so many things. And they tell me they just don't have time to go to Mass. I'm worried. I don't think my daughter and her husband are interested in Catholicism at all. And they are not teaching my grandchildren anything about it."

The grandfather feels the pain and asks, "Is it my fault? Did I do something wrong? I tried really hard, and now they don't go to Mass at all. And my grandchildren are getting nothing. I'm worried."

Like this man, grandparents can feel like they missed their opportunity. Their own children are grown now and have lost some or all interest in the Church.

Then the grandfather asks, "What can I do about it?"

I respond, "Well done! You're asking exactly the right question."

What can I do about it? Is this your question? Are you worried about your grandchild(ren)? Are you concerned their future will not include the Catholic faith, or any faith at all? Does it pain you to see all the obstacles the world places in the path of your grandchild and the Church?

I have good news. That pain you're feeling is a gift from God.

In this book, I will show you why God gives you that pain and what you can do about it. You can use it for good. It's a gift. In fact, it's a vocation. God made you to be a grandparent.

If you are a new grandparent, God is giving you a new vocation. If you are a seasoned grandparent, God invites you to get really clear on what your role means and why He gave you this vocation in the first place.

Like you, I have been observing and am deeply worried about the culture where our grandchildren will grow—and are growing—up. In many ways, it is a toxic place. We know there is something wrong but no one seems able to fix it. The saturation of sexual messages. The instability. The widespread violence. The lack of respect for other human beings. Illegitimacy. Abused children. Neglect. The cruelty and isolation often created by social media. The hostility toward, and even mockery of, our Church and our Catholic faith.

I imagine you worry like I do. Watching children grow up today feels a lot like watching a James Bond movie in which the bad guy has kidnapped a girl and is waiting to kill her at the end of a slow-moving conveyor belt. At times, it feels like your grandchildren have been placed on the culture's conveyor belt. That belt empties into a huge wood chipper where lives, relationships, and futures are churned up and spit out. And your gut is telling you to do something to prevent that from happening to your grandchild—fast, before the bad guy wins.

That is why I wrote this book. This book is for you, and for me.

This book is for us because the battle for our grandchildren has already begun. Whoever wants them the most will get them. This is a fight you can win.

Don't Waste Your Pain

If you are feeling that pain as you watch your grandchildren growing up separated from the Catholic Church, please know it is sending an important message. If it hurts you to watch our culture growing ever more toxic, please know that pain is good. Yes, it is a good thing that it's painful. That pain in your soul exists because there is a lot at stake. It is the first step on your journey.

What is your pain telling you? First, it is God getting your attention. C. S. Lewis used to say that pain is God's megaphone to get our attention in the middle of all the noise of our lives. God whispers to us in our pleasures. He shouts to us in our pain.

Remember Jonah and the whale. Jonah wants to go another direction from where God wants him to go. When God wants to get Jonah's attention, He sends him on a cruise in the belly of a whale. After three days in that belly, at the bottom of the sea, Jonah finally says, "When my soul fainted within me, I remembered the Lord" (Jonah 2:7). Finally, God has Jonah's attention—in the pain.

Second, that pain means you have a choice: to do something or to do nothing. God is nudging you. He is calling you through that uncomfortable pain in your soul. He is inviting you out of the pain and into something deeper and truer. Trust Him.

God can bring purpose out of the pain you are feeling. He not only can, but He will. God hopes to use that pain to do significant things in your life and in the lives of the people around you.

Very simply, God is nudging you forward. He is calling you into action. You have a role to play.

God allows pain for all kinds of reasons. Sometimes the pain results from dumb choices we make—for instance, when we put our hand on the burner of a hot stove. Sometimes God allows pain so that you and I will learn to depend on Him and trust Him more deeply. Sometimes we learn something very deep through our pain. If you never had a problem, you would never realize just how much you need God. Without pain, you and I might think we were self-sufficient. Sometimes God allows pain because He wants to give you or me a task. He often allows pain in my life to give me the opportunity to serve other people. Pain makes us humble and sensitive to the needs of others and also to the nudging of God.

God never wastes a hurt—but you can waste it if you do not learn from it or share it. God invites you to use your pain to help someone else. He wants to redeem your pain.

St. John Paul II said, "Don't waste your suffering." In other words, put your suffering to work for your own salvation, for your family, and for the kingdom of God. Suffering offered to Christ is precious to our Lord. Don't waste it. Offer it up with Christ for the salvation of your grandchildren's souls.

Your calling is emerging from God. He nudges you in your pain to do something. To dream big. To serve bigger.

Don't waste your pain. Use it.

Grandparent Dreams

Dream. That's what grandparents do. Grandparents dream deep dreams for their families. Grandfathers hold longings and desires for the grandchildren who carry their names. Grandmothers harbor hopes for the future of their families and the faith of their grandchildren.

Grandparents dream and hope. It's what they do; it's just who they are.

Grandmothers and grandfathers hope for:

- healthy bodies and futures for their grandchildren
- excellent education of their grandchildren's minds to think and create like God intends
- thriving marriages and relationships for the family's generations to come
- vibrant faith inspired by the beauty and genius of Catholicism
- all their family to come to happiness with Jesus in this life and in the world to come

These grandparent dreams come from God. He planted them in you.

Yet, too many just haven't thought about their vocation as grandparents very much. Few grandparents I meet are intentional about what they really want and what they will actually do for their grandchildren. They just kind of let it happen.

Worse, the temptation is to focus on the wrong things, to have misplaced priorities. Ask yourself: If you had the choice between your grandchild having a great career and your grandchild having a great faith, which would you choose? What does your answer to that question teach you about yourself?

God dreams for more. After all, a lot is at stake: your family.

Your Deepest Desires

You may want to **pass the torch**. The teachings of Catholicism have shaped every part of your life. You grew up in a Catholic home and a Catholic family. You and your siblings attended Catholic school. Your friends were Catholic and your sports teams were Catholic. Being Catholic has helped shape everything you have done: your marriage, your job, your family, your friends, your community. And you have benefited from the richness and principles of Catholicism. You want to pass that same torch to your grandchildren so that they can carry it for the next generation, because you know it leads to happiness, both here and in eternity.

Or perhaps you want to **light the fire**. Somewhere along the way, you figured it out. You connected the dots. You had been taught all about the Mass and the sacraments. You had learned lots of the *Catechism*. You had prayed the rosary hundreds of times. But it had never really clicked. Until one day you read a great Catholic book, or were inspired by a remarkable homily, or listened to a moving talk on CD, and it all came together. Suddenly, your spirit came alive and you really *got* it. You experienced the power of the faith and the love of Christ firsthand, deep within you. And you have never been the same. Something lit the fire in you, and you want to help light that same fire in your grandchildren. You want them to have what you have: passion and purpose.

Or maybe your goal is simply to **help your grandchildren be happy**. You learned early on that God created us for happiness. And you have discovered in your life that it is extremely difficult, if not impossible, to find happiness apart from God. Life just doesn't work without God in it. You want your grandchildren to be happy, so you deeply yearn to pour the foundation for their lives. Because you know that God will help them become loving, compassionate, and good. He will guide them to become the-best-version-of-themselves.

Finally, you might envision your own future. Ultimately, you hope to be with God in heaven. The ancient Jews had a name for Him: the Place. God is the Place. You and I were made by God to **get to the Place**, to get to Him. You hope to get to the Place, and you really want to help your grandchildren get there too. Death is not the end; it's the beginning. Death transitions us to new life with God, and you want your grandchildren to be there with you forever.

You may hope for one of these, or you may hope for all of them. To pass the torch of Catholicism. To light the fire of faith. To lay the foundation for a happy life. To help your grandchildren get to God, the Place. All these desires come from God. He puts them in you because He has great hopes for your family too. And He has given you this vocation so that you can work with Him to make it happen.

To make it happen, you will need a plan. And in this book, I will teach you how to map out that plan, step by step, to work with God to make these dreams come true.

I don't know how this book landed in your hands. You might have purchased it on your own. Perhaps a friend recommended it or you received it as a gift from your parish, or perhaps a leader chose it for a group discussion. But you owe the person who got you this book a debt of gratitude. They have served you powerfully. Say a prayer for him or her right now. Their kindness will alter the future of your family.

God has given you and me a great opportunity. Grandparents today are more important than ever before. Failure is not an option.

How to Use This Book

In this book, I will:

- discuss the research that proves you are a vital influencer and predictor of your grandchild's spiritual future
- share the single most important question to ask your grandchild
- teach you the most crucial spiritual habit to cultivate in your family's life
- define success as a Catholic grandparent and how to take steps to create it
- tell you what you need to stop doing
- tell you what you need to start doing

As you read and use this book, begin with the end in mind. Remember your goal: for your grandchildren to live the best life imaginable. Because you know they were made for happiness with God and that there is no such thing as a great life apart from Him. Because you want them to know Jesus and to get to heaven. They were made for greatness.

Frankly, I invite you to have a vision even larger than that. Often we in the Church care about youth ministry only when our own teenagers are in it, or we give to the Catholic school only when our own children are attending. We operate out of a spiritual consumerism. But God is calling you and me to care for all grandchildren. Jesus came for them all, whether yours, mine, or those of someone we've never met. You and I have a role to play in helping the Church reach every grandchild.

That's why I am here. Our entire team at Dynamic Catholic exists to serve the Church. We want to help the Church be better for all God's people and their grandchildren. In fact, your grandchild will be shaped and influenced by all kinds of people. Begin praying now for the person who will reengage your grandson when he drifts or inspire your granddaughter when she wanders.

There are two ways to read and use this book. You may wish to read it in one fell swoop. And that is good. But I believe you will find it even more helpful to read it one chapter at a time, digesting each point, each life-changing habit, and each empowering action step.

Part one of this book will illustrate just how important you are. You play a crucial role in the life and choices of your grandchild. And God has given you this important vocation for a reason.

In part two, I will guide you step by step to develop your own personal plan to make your dreams for your grandchild come true. Best of all, each chapter provides an effective Action Step. This is your specific takeaway that you can begin doing right now. Grab on to it and start today.

For this book, I have spoken to hundreds of grandparents across the country. I have intensively studied the scientific and developmental research around the role and influence of grandparents. And I have applied my thirty years of experience in full-time ministry with families. All of this will help you arrive at your deepest dream of all: what God Himself desires for your family.

At Dynamic Catholic, we like to say, "Our lives change when

our habits change." Working your way through each chapter and absorbing these key tools will allow you to form your own plan for life-changing family habits. I have been helping families and individuals build excellent habits for more than thirty years. And in this book I will help you do that too!

Grandchildren are the stars in your crown. It is time for them to shine now and forever.

You can do this. In fact, we will do it together.

===

Key Point
This book is designed to help you dream God's dreams with your grandchild and to make those dreams a reality.

Question to Consider
When you envision the future of your grandchild, what do you see for him or her at age eighteen, age twenty-five, age fifty?

Action Step
Craft an ABCs of Dreams for your grandchild modeled after the one below. Begin to dream.

Prayer
Lord, help me to dream your dreams for me and for my family. Amen.

One Helpful Tool
The ABCs of Dreams

When little Allen Joseph arrived, I began to dream in a new way, for a new generation in our family, our first grandchild. After his birth, I wrote some of my dreams and hopes for his life and for his faith.

Dear Allen Joseph:

Your grandmother and I have deep dreams for you. These are my ABCs of Dreams for you.

A good priest: Is there anything better for a boy, a teen, and a man to have in his life? May you always have a good priest in your life.

Baptism: My eyes will fill with tears when my daughter holds you to receive the waters of baptism. What a gift! New life in the family of God. All the possibilities. May you not only know *who* you are but also *whose* you are.

Caring teachers: The greatest gift we can give you is the gift of faith. I pray for caring teachers throughout your life to show you the way and to help you embrace it.

Deep love for people: Jesus teaches us to do two things: (1) Love God; and (2) love people. I am not concerned with whether you attain wealth or recognition. May you be known most of all for your deep, deep love.

Easter people: After all, that *is* who we are. One man said, "If you don't believe in the Resurrection, then you're not a believer." We are Easter people. I hope you will learn to look forward with desire and confidence. With that, you will have a hope that the world does not.

Funerals: May you be inspired by funerals because we are Easter people.

Great education: I hope you have a fine mind. Even more so, I hope for an education that truly prepares you for life—to think fully, to have the "mind of Christ."

Heart for God: I pray you will be like King David, a man after God's own heart.

Inspiring music: May your ear be filled with the melody of God. Whether it be "In Christ Alone," "Be Thou My Vision," or a tune I have not yet heard.

Jesus on the crucifix: When I sit and listen to my friend as he musters every ounce of courage to endure chemo treatments, he and I look at the crucifix, to our suffering Lord. I pray, my grandson, that you experience that same hope in your own times of confusion, pain, or despair.

Knowing where you are headed: Our citizenship is in heaven. An old Jewish Hebrew name for God is the Place. I want you to know that's where we are going. You are destined to be in Him. God is our Place.

Love: It has always defined the Church and God's people. Love separates us from the world. We love. That will make you different.

Monastery of the Holy Spirit: I spend a retreat day there each month. The sheer beauty of the architecture in the church alone lifts my heart. I hope to share that same inspiration with you very soon.

Not alone: You are not alone, ever. We are surrounded by a great cloud of witnesses, people of mission who lived life well. We shall meet them face-to-face when we too reach the Place.

Outstanding sense of vocation and purpose: Whether you are called to be a priest or to single or married life, I pray for you to embrace a life filled with divine purpose. May that purpose animate your world every day.

Parents: When I see parents sitting with their children at Mass, praying with their kids in a restaurant, or serving on a mission team as a family, I sense the deepest hope imaginable. Those parents get it—they are investing in their kids' souls. And that will make all the difference. May God bless your parents as they seek to do the same for you.

Quests: Think St. John Fisher, who was willing to lose everything, even his life, in his quest to love God and to be obedient. Quests will remind you, my little boy, that you can be better and better. And you will be.

Reception into the Church: Who can be at the Easter Vigil Mass and witness a young man affirming his faithful desire to become a part of the Easter people and not feel hope? I look forward to the day you fully enter the Church.

St. Gertrude the Great: What a woman! I hope you get to know her a bit in your life. She's the only female saint to be called "the Great," and it's easy to see why. Read her prayer and it becomes obvious. She is a lady of great hope.

O Sacred Heart of Jesus, fountain of eternal life, Your Heart is a glowing furnace of Love. You are my refuge and my sanctuary. O my adorable and loving Savior, consume my heart with the burning fire with which Yours is aflamed. Pour down on my soul those graces which flow from Your love. Let my heart be united with Yours.

The Eucharist: The Body. The Blood. The Eucharist changed my life and my soul. I hope it will feed and nourish you every day of your life.

Unconditional love: For just a moment, meeting you, my grandson, drew me into the heart of God, a heart filled with unconditional love. If I, as a flawed earthly grandfather, can love you like that, I can only begin to imagine how much God's unconditional love abounds for you.

Very generous people: People who give are great dreamers. People of possibility. May you become one of them.

Work ethic: Everyone in your family seems to have a great one. I hope you get one too. No task is too small or too large to offer to God.

X, the first letter for Christ in the original Greek: X is a symbol for Christ in the early Church. The dictionary says "hope" is a person in whom expectations are centered. For you, my grandson, I pray that person will be Jesus. After all, He is the Christ.

You remind me I am not alone: I will help you discover that we are on this journey to dream together with many good people.

Zephyr: A fresh wind. There is one blowing in the Church—can you feel it? May it inspire your life today, tomorrow, and forever. Amen.

Love,
Your Dreaming Grandpa

2. WHY YOU MATTER (EVEN MORE THAN YOU KNOW)

Grandparents are a family's greatest treasure,
The founders of a loving legacy, the greatest storytellers,
The keepers of traditions that linger on in cherished memory.
Grandparents are the family's strong foundation.

—Author unknown

Only a small group of elite athletes make it to Kilimanjaro's 19,341-foot summit in Tanzania. The ascent covers thirty-eight miles. The journey is grueling.

Mt. Kilimanjaro is not for quitters.

Kyle's Grandmother

When Kyle Maynard reached the top of Mount Kilimanjaro in 2012, he and his entire team of climbers beamed with pride. At that moment, I imagine the first person Kyle thought about was his grandmother.

Kyle Maynard has no hands or feet. Doctors call his condition congenital amputation. That means he was born with legs that end at his knees, and arms that end at his elbows. Yet somehow Kyle became the first quadruple amputee to reach the peak of Kiliman-jaro, and he did it without the help of prosthetics. He bear-crawled on the trail ten days to mount that summit. That takes courage.

Four years later, Kyle conquered Mount Aconcagua in Argentina, the highest mountain in the Western and Southern Hemispheres. This one stands 22,841 feet and can be deadly. Again, at the top, I bet Kyle's first thoughts turned to his grandmother.

As you can imagine, Kyle had an extraordinarily challenging childhood. Being born with no hands and feet means lots of awkward stares and cruel teasing. But most of all, it creates great physical hardship.

Kyle's body has only three major joints: his neck and two shoulders. Yet, over time, he learned not only to move on his own but also to type fifty words a minute, to write impeccably, and to eat with silverware, all without assistance. Meanwhile, he also became a champion wrestler in Georgia with his unique style, using his head like a battering ram and his limbs like clubs. That's fortitude.

From the moment of Kyle's birth, his parents and his grand-parents showered him with love and encouragement. His grand-mother, Grandma Betty, proved especially influential. She possessed a deep faith in God, and she invested abundantly in passing that faith on to Kyle.

Grandma Betty often took Kyle to the grocery store, where he would meet the stares and comments of surprised fellow shoppers. During one of those grocery visits, Kyle asked, "Grandma, why am I different from other kids?"

Her answer: "God made you special, Kyle, and it's okay to be different. No two people are ever going to be exactly the same."

As Kyle struggled with feeling different and desiring to be accepted, Grandma Betty consistently reassured him that God loved him fully and completely. She encouraged him to be friendly and to introduce himself to the people around him. Slowly, Grandma Betty and the family built Kyle's faith and confidence so that he could survive the rigors of school, social life, and sports as a boy, and then as a man, without hands and feet. Those lessons from his grandmother gave him the foundation on which to build his life. In fact, Kyle gives motivational talks, sharing his grandmother's wisdom with others to help keep her spirit alive.

So it only makes sense that his first thoughts at the top of Mount Kilimanjaro were prayers of thanksgiving to God for the success of the journey and for the gift of his grandmother. Her investments in him had paid off in ways neither she nor Kyle could ever have imagined.

Only You

God has a vision for your family; He didn't create us to be alone. The family is the foundation of civilization, the basic building block of any stable society. If you want to predict the future of a society, watch the direction families are moving in that society. Are they becoming more stable or more chaotic? Is there more love or more disarray in families?

You and I first experience the love of God in our original community of love, our family. Your family was and is your first experience of not being alone. Your first experience of love, whether positive or negative, comes from your family. Family gives your life roots, a home base.

Never underestimate how deep those roots are and how strong the draw of family is. The bond is so strong that even it if is tattered and unhealthy, children feel the bond and are pulled back to it. Family is our roots. The older we get the more we think about our roots. In a healthy family, we are loved and accepted regardless of what we have done or what we have or who we are in the world's eyes. Family, like love, is built on acceptance.

Even children from the most dysfunctional of homes—filled with addiction, poor choices, and chaos—still feel a deep and powerful attraction back to those roots.

Family provides the primary cell or foundation for the Church, just as it does for society. If we learn the faith at home, we have our greatest chance to thrive. The family becomes our community, where we help each other become the-best-version-of-ourselves. And lots of wonderful things come with that: love, boundaries, safety, correction, encouragement, and accountability.

When it comes to family, grandparents matter, a lot. No one can show love, nurturing, and encouragement like a grandparent. Researchers at Oxford University and Boston College have found that children are shaped by their grandparents in deeply significant ways. Those who spend time with their grandparents tend to have fewer emotional and behavioral problems and typically do better in social settings. Like Kyle Maynard, they also tend to have higher self-esteem.

Grandparents give unconditional love and support. They offer advice and problem-solving and share their skills and passions. And they provide a safe and trusted refuge away from parents. An extensive study at Oxford found clear links between involved grandparents and adolescent well-being. Quite simply, actively engaging with your grandchildren will bear great fruit.

Your love teaches your grandchildren to love and be loved. It helps them feel confident and secure in the world. Your love builds the foundation for your grandchildren's happy life.

Faith Drives Happiness

That foundation for your grandchildren's happy life is directly linked to their having an active religious faith. The research points out just how important faith is to a young person's life. The National Study of Youth and Religion (NSYR) at Notre Dame and University of North Carolina at Chapel Hill shows important findings about a healthy, satisfying life. Pay attention to this.

Adolescents with an active personal religious faith are more likely to:

- have positive attitudes toward themselves
- feel like their lives are useful and meaningful
- feel hopeful about their futures
- feel satisfied with their lives
- feel like they have something to be proud of
- feel it's good to be alive
- enjoy being in school

When teenagers lack religious faith, they search for meaning (and love) wherever they think they might find it—and too often that is in risky behaviors like reckless driving, casual sex, and substance abuse.

In other words, if you want your grandchild to have a good life, then an active religious faith is the straightest path to it. It is hard to find happiness without God. After all, we Catholics know "our hearts are restless until they rest in God," as St. Augustine said.

And that journey toward faith and happiness starts early on in your grandchild's life. This is where you come into the picture in a profound way.

Recent research, led by Dr. Lisa Miller at Columbia University's Teachers College, has demonstrated that we are all biologically wired for a spiritual connection from the very start of life. That comes as no surprise to us Catholics. After all, we know well that we were made by God, for God, and in the image of God.

Miller's research makes a startling discovery: When a parent and child have the same deep personal relationship with a religion, that faith sharing produces richer protection for the child against depression, alcohol abuse, and risk taking than any other factor.

There is only one factor even greater than a parent and child's shared faith in seeking to shield a child from some of the perils of life: when the *grandparent*, parent, and child have the same deep personal relationship with the religion.

Child, parent, and *grandparent*, sharing the same deep faith, practicing it together. It is a game changer. Grandparents are vital in laying the foundation for happy lives.

Miller's research leads to this basic truth: A firm faith foundation in place begins in childhood. That faith and spiritual life can then be supported in the challenging years of adolescence as the child's spirituality deepens. Nourished through adolescence, it can then become the crucial tool for health and healing in adult life. In other words, a faith-filled childhood leads to the greatest likelihood of navigating adolescence well. That then leads to the greatest likelihood of leading a healthy adult life.

Faith drives happiness. And grandparents help drive faith.

How Faith Emerges

If you want your grandchildren to discover, learn, and embrace the faith to prepare them for adolescence and adulthood, how does that actually happen?

First, children whose grandparents share and live the Catholic faith with them tend to have the highest likelihood of attending Mass and being Catholic when they become adults.

When it comes to grandparent involvement, the stakes are high when you look at God and how our spiritual lives take shape.

The results from the research at Columbia can be summarized in four key points. When it comes to embracing the faith, the clearest and best path will have you:

1. Learn the faith early from your family.
2. Practice the faith regularly in your childhood.
3. Stay connected to an encouraging community of believers.
4. Allow this foundation to help carry you through the turbulence of adolescence.

Like learning to speak and to read, your grandchild's faith is best built in childhood. When holy moments and experiences with God are built into the first thirteen years of life, that faith is available to help the adolescent decide who, and what kind of person, he or she wants to be. Spirituality, supported in childhood, prepares an adolescent for the critical moments and decisions we all face as we enter our teenage years.

This makes sense because it is also true in so many other parts of our lives.

We are all born with a capacity for math, but you do not want to wait until you are a teenager to begin to learn math. Instead, you begin with the basics as a child. You learn your numbers. Then you learn to count. Then you figure out how to add and subtract. With that in place, you can take the leap to multiplication and division. As you enter adolescence, with your solid mathematical foundation supporting you, you can then approach the more rigorous and complex subjects of algebra and geometry. No one begins math from scratch by learning to count at age fourteen. It would be almost impossible. No parent says, "I am not going to teach my child math. I am going to let them decide what they want to learn when they want to learn it."

Math is mastered by learning the basics, practicing them over and over again, and doing so early in life. The need for the basics and for a solid math foundation in childhood is clear. Without that foundation, the more complex mathematical subjects are impossible to master.

Or, for comparison, look at a sport. It is much easier to learn to play golf when you are young than when you are older. You are born with basic physical movement. You begin at an early age to develop your fine motor skills. Then you discover how to crawl, walk, run, and jump as you grow. With those skills in place, you can move on to basic skills of golf as you learn how to swing the club. You make more progress as you then learn how to hit the ball cleanly, judge distances, develop touch, and embrace the basic language of the game. Tiger Woods learned these essential skills so well by age three that he shot a 48 on the back nine of the Navy golf course. At age three!

As you continue to grow and mature in your skills, you begin to understand your coach. The game begins to make more and more sense to you. You can see the nuances and the angles of the game. Finally, your adolescent mind starts to frame the larger picture of how the various parts of the game all fit together. Your thirst for learning, your practice, and your growth in skills all flow nicely into a mastering of the sport.

By acquiring these basic skills early on, you can then refine and enrich what you are doing in order to develop a full and complete game as an adult. Very few great golfers began golf later in life. If you were to wait until age twenty-five to pick up a club for the very first time, you would already be years behind. More important, you would be scrambling to absorb these lessons into a mind that has already developed its own ways of thinking and a body that has already developed its own ways of moving and doing.

Learning new things becomes slower and more challenging as we age. This is true for virtually any sport. Begin when you are young, build the basics, practice and discover, and then mature into mastery.

As it is with math or golf, so too is it with faith.

A young child naturally seeks out a healthy, inspiring spiritual life. We are just made that way. A child loves to learn and explore. A child enjoys carefree timelessness to explore the world, play with ideas, and imagine possibilities. Some of that exploration takes place in the physical world, and some of it takes place in the spiritual world.

Here's the good news: Early spiritual life usually begins with the child's relationships with family members, as those family members represent and embody the love of God. It is through close family members that a child first experiences love. And it is often in that love that a child begins to embrace the idea of a loving God who cares immensely about him or her. Developmentally speaking, early love sets the child on a path to faith.

How does this early love occur? The great gift you can provide your grandchild early on is the gift of your time and your undivided attention. Careful listening and conversation demonstrates that you love a child and that she or he matters.

In an increasingly distracted smartphone world, it is often a grandparent who actually sits and listens attentively to a child's questions. In a hurry-scurry life, a grandparent can play for hours on end with a grandchild, giving precious undivided attention that communicates love. A grandparent frequently welcomes a child's feelings and is willing to have long, deep talks. All of these simple actions embody love and place the child on a path that leads to God.

It is important to realize that science confirms what the Church has been teaching us all along: If you want your grandchildren to have a good life, then help them build an active, personal religious faith. And if you want them to develop a full, healthy faith life, it is important to start early. That is the clearest path to becoming the-best-version-of-themselves. Grandparents can make all the difference.

But how do you do that?

Start Early. And Often.

Here is where it gets really real.

Research from the Barna Group shows we have a crucial window, from birth to age thirteen, to shape the spiritual life of a child. By the age of thirteen, a child's spiritual identity is largely set in place. Essentially, by that age, the spiritual foundation has been poured and is beginning to dry. You are most likely to be a Catholic adult if you have embraced the Catholic faith in a personal way by this time. If you love Jesus and His Church by then, your spiritual foundation is very likely to carry you through your adult life.

Likewise, if a person does not have that Catholic Christian foundation by age thirteen, an enormous amount of makeup work lies ahead for them in their teenage years. They can still get the foundation poured, but it is going to take considerable work. Just like a teenager will face challenges if he enrolls in algebra without knowing addition and subtraction, he will find it challenging to figure out life and purpose if he has not had meaningful spiritual experiences beforehand. That initial window of opportunity from birth to age thirteen makes all the difference.

In other words, the earlier, the better. The sooner and more frequently you can help your grandchild have spiritual experiences and holy moments (more on how to do this will follow in the coming chapters), the more likely your grandchild is to be Catholic not only as a teenager but also as an adult.

Remember again the first key finding from Miller's research at Columbia regarding how faith is most likely to be embraced by a person: **They need to learn it early from their family**. As a grandparent, that means you. You are family.

And the second finding: **They must practice it in their childhood**. As a grandparent, that means start early and walk alongside your grandchild all throughout their childhood. There is no substitute for your early and frequent displays of love, attention, and faith.

The life of Sister Ruth illustrates this. When Sister Ruth died, friends and family attended the funeral Mass for this beautiful eighty-five-year-old nun. She had faithfully lived as a cloistered Dominican sister all her adult life. She was prayerful, loving, and devoted.

At the funeral, the priest shared a story from Sister Ruth's childhood. Her family loved the Sacred Heart of Jesus. In fact, they had a picture of it in their den over the fireplace mantel, right smack in the center of the wall where everyone saw it all the time.

One weekend, the family attended Mass at their parish. The priest's homily shared the beautiful love of God as he described the Sacred Heart of Jesus. When the family came home, they ate lunch together. A few minutes later, when the parents walked into the den, they found little seven-year-old Ruth kneeling in front of that picture of the Sacred Heart. She was whispering over and over, "Lord Jesus, I will love you forever."

And she did exactly that. Sister Ruth devoted her entire life to Jesus, just as He had devoted Himself to her. She knew it by age seven.

How many experiences of that loving heart of Jesus she must have had as a child to make that simple prayer of devotion to Him by the age of seven! And how deeply she already knew by then what mattered most in her life and what mattered least—so much so that the decisions she made then shaped every single day of the rest of her life.

Faith grows and ripens in a developmental process, just like the language, math, and athletic skills we first learn as children. In childhood, we learn and explore the basics; the foundation is poured so that the house can be built. Don't miss the window God has opened in each child to experience His love from the very beginning of life.

Grandma Betty encouraged and loved Kyle Maynard from his earliest moments. Her faith inspired him to embrace the faith and even to climb Kilimanjaro against all odds. She helped light the fire of faith deep within him early on.

Your grandparent love and your grandparent faith can make all the difference. In fact, it *will* make all the difference. You matter. It's a fact.

Key Point

Only you can do what you can do. Grandparents are crucial.

Question to Consider

Do you remember your own experience with a grandparent? How has it shaped you?

Action Step

Examine the present. What kind of grandparent are you now? Does it match up with who you want to be?

Prayer

Lord, help me to lay the foundation for my grandchildren. Help me to fulfill my vocation. Show me the way forward. Amen.

One Helpful Tool
Prayer of a Grandfather

Lord
You have now given me the privilege
Of my own family

Help me to accept with humility
This sacred gift

May I be gentle and strong
Knowing right from wrong
May I be firm yet fair

May my wife find in me
A companion for life
A true friend
A kind listener
May my grandchildren know
Protection
Affection
Direction

May I open for them
The book of knowledge
The secret doorway to adventure
May the child in me always
    accompany the child in them

May I hold them in times of fear
May I dry the eyes that cry soft tears
May we journey together through
    many years

Lord, may they know You
Because of me
Your consoling compassionate way
Woven through life each day

May I be silent when I need to hear
Affirm
And gently steer
The anxious heart to a place of calm

Lord, may I be blessed in my
    children's children
May my wonder never cease
May I find with self-acceptance
The gift of inner peace

May I rest with quiet contentment
And make this silent prayer
Father of all Fathers
Guide our earthly way
Amen.

(Adapted from Fr. Liam Lawton, *Hope Prayer*)

3. YOUR SUCCESS DEFINED

You have made us for yourself, O Lord,
and our hearts are restless until they rest in You.
—St. Augustine

When each of our two daughters was baptized, our dear friends gave us a framed picture of Jesus smiling and holding small children. Anita and I hung those pictures, one in each of our girls' bedrooms, right over their beds.

Because of that gift from friends, our daughters grew up each night of their lives with Jesus watching and smiling over them as they slept.

Our Dream

The significance of this gift became clear when SarahAnn, our older daughter, was preparing to leave for college. That meant our first-born would be walking out the door into a new season of her life. A season of independence and exploration. A season when her parents would not be waiting for her at home each evening, when we would not be looking over her shoulder each day. SarahAnn would walk out with big hopes and dreams and also with fears and worries. Leaving home for the first time is a huge step. Everything changes.

On the evening before her departure for school, we all knew this last night together at home represented a lot. The four of us decided to spend the evening together as a family—no friends, no visitors. This was our last night with things the way they were. The next day, we would drive SarahAnn off to college and things would be different. Only three of us would still be at home.

SarahAnn would be setting out on a new adventure, living in the world and exploring things like a college student does. When she came home, she now would be more like a guest and a grown-up. Things would be different. We all knew that.

So, on that last night with her at home, we ate dinner together, played games, and just talked. We wanted to savor every bit of this time. Tomorrow things would change, and there would be no going back to the way they used to be.

As the evening drew to a close, SarahAnn got up and said, "I think I am going to go on to bed. Tomorrow is a big day, and I want to get a little sleep to be ready." We all nodded, and she went upstairs to her bedroom.

An hour or two later, I said something similar. "Tomorrow is a big day. Since I am the only man in this family, I'll be doing most of the moving and lifting as we take her stuff to school. So I am going to go on to bed and get some rest so I will be ready."

As I prepared for bed, I told Anita, "I think I will check on SarahAnn and tell her good night."

I walked down the hall to SarahAnn's room and knocked on the door. No answer. I assumed she was asleep, so I slowly opened the door and peeked in.

There she was, asleep on the bed, her arms wrapped tightly around the picture of the smiling Jesus, pulling it close to her chest.

I knew right then. She was going to be just fine.

She knew Him. And she knew He held her future. She was ready.

Today each of our grandsons has a picture, carefully hung over his bed, of smiling Jesus holding small children. They will grow up knowing that Jesus is watching over them every day of their lives. They will know who holds their future.

That is our dream.

God Is the Place

You love the Catholic faith. You have experienced the genius of Catholicism. You embrace the beauty of the faith. Being Catholic has made your life better. Your relationships are better because you are Catholic. You approach work differently because you are Catholic. You make decisions with different values in mind because you are Catholic. You organize your time in a unique way because you are Catholic.

Very simply, you feel rich because you are Catholic. And you want your grandchildren to feel that richness too.

Right now, you would like your grandchildren to go to Mass. Because Catholicism has changed your life and you have big dreams for your family that cannot be attained without the Catholic faith. And it begins with Mass, doesn't it?

You want your family's life to be sustained by the presence of God because you know they are going to need it in trying times. In life's toughest times, in those moments that reveal who you are in the deepest way, faith will make the difference.

You want more for them than this world offers. You know that our culture right now is toxic. You are worried about sending your grandchildren into the chaos and confusion of this world.

You hope your grandchild will be nourished by the Eucharist in the same way you have been.

You desire for your grandchildren to be strengthened through prayer, knowing the hand of God each day of their lives. You have that assurance, and you dream of that for them too.

You are headed to heaven, the Place, and you want to greet your children and grandchildren there too.

This is what success looks like. And what I would like you to know is that you are the guide. You are the mapmaker for that dream to come true. You can help guide your grandchildren to the Place. You can lead them on the way home. You can prepare the map, and walk alongside them so that they find the path for themselves.

This is your dream. This is success.

Preparing Your Family for the Toughest Times

When the Israelites were about to enter the Promised Land, Moses was clear about what the dream was. He knew Israel was entering a new stage of life. Finally, after years of wandering, they were about to possess the very promise of God. This was an important moment. And he wanted to be sure they remembered the dream.

So Moses gave them clear direction:

This then is the commandment, the statutes and the ordinances, which the Lord, your God, has commanded that you be taught to observe in the land you are about to cross into to possess, so that you, that is, you, *your child, and your grandchild*, may fear the Lord, your God, by keeping, as long as you live, all his statutes and commandments which I enjoin on you, and thus have long life. (Deuteronomy 6:1–2, NAB, emphasis added)

Moses wants them to help their kids and grandkids find and get to God.

Then, he teaches them *how* to train their grandchildren to discover and remain in God.

Hear, O Israel: The Lord our God is one Lord; and you shall *love the Lord* your God with all your heart, and with all your soul, and with all your might.

And these words which I command you this day shall be upon your heart; and you shall teach them diligently to your children, and shall *talk of them when you sit in your house, and when you walk by the way, and when you lie down and when you rise. And you shall bind them as a sign upon your hand, and they shall be as frontlets between your eyes. And you shall write them on the doorposts of your house and on your gates.* (Deuteronomy 6:4–9, emphasis added)

Moses says two key things. First: Love the Lord. Completely— with all your heart, with all your soul, with all your might.

Second: Be sure to teach your children and grandchildren to do the same. Talk about God's commandments with your family. Talk about them when you walk, when you sit, when you lie down, when you get up. Talk about them all the time. Write them on your hand. Put them on your forehead. Write them on your doors and on your gates. May the words of God be part of your conversation every day.

In other words, focus on the main thing. Dial in to what matters most. Keep it in front of you all the time. Never let it slip your mind.

Love God. Do what He tells you to do. And do everything you can to help your children and grandchildren do that too. Worship God. Pray. Give thanks to Him. Honor Him with your work and your relationships. Invite Him to be a part of everything you do.

Moses knew tough times lay ahead. The Israelites would not be greeted warmly by everyone they met. Armies would oppose them. Weather would not always cooperate. Crops would not always arrive. Food would often be scarce. The Israelites would need to remember the dream.

It was not about them. It was all about God. It was not merely about the present. It was all about the future. And Moses wanted to be sure they knew that. Because they would need that dream when they hit life's toughest moments. Love God completely. Teach your children and your grandchildren to love Him too. Because the time will come when you really need Him, and only your faith will carry you.

Moses' words still ring true today. Tough times will arrive for every person, every family. And when those challenges come, only faith will carry you.

I learned that lesson again when I walked into our church one Tuesday with a heavy heart and a sad spirit.

We had lost dear little Anna, a fellow parishioner, barely nine years old, who died after nine difficult months suffering with leukemia. As we grieved that morning, we prayed, we sang, we shared Scripture, and we shared the Eucharist, the meal of life.

Then her grandfather made his way to the microphone. He wanted to share little Anna's favorite Bible story with us. He and Anna had read it together dozens, maybe hundreds of times.

Anna never let anyone read this story to her. She always insisted on reading it aloud herself.

So he began to read from a children's Bible, the one that had belonged to Anna:

During the forty days after Jesus' resurrection, Jesus appeared to his disciples from time to time. He spoke to them about the kingdom of God.

Once he told them to stay in Jerusalem and wait for the gift he would send them. That gift would be the Holy Spirit. He would live in them and guide them. He would be a Comforter to them. Jesus wanted them to tell everyone on earth that he had died for them. He told them to teach and to baptize those who believed.

After Jesus said this, he was taken up to heaven right in front of their eyes. A cloud hid him from their sight and two angels, who looked like men dressed in white, came and stood beside them.

The angels said, "Why are you looking up in the sky? This same Jesus who has been taken up into heaven will come back some day in the same way you have seen him go into heaven."

We also believe that he will come again.

As Anna's grandfather finished reading this story, his eyes welled with tears. He told us that each time Anna had read this passage to him, when she was finished, she looked directly at him. At first, she looked with questioning eyes. But over time, her eyes turned knowing.

She knew. Little Anna really, really knew.

As her grandfather shared this experience with us, at that moment, the atmosphere in the church was so thick I could barely see. I could not move. Frankly, I was transfixed. At that moment, all around me was a cloud; the place was filled with the glory of God.

A little nine-year-old girl, speaking through her grandfather, had reminded me. In fact, Anna had reminded all of us. Jesus will live in us and comfort us. And He will indeed come again. She had learned it by reading the Scriptures with her grandfather, and in the end, she was teaching it back to him.

Little Anna knew: In life's toughest moments, our faith will make all the difference. God alone will see us through.

Every family needs to know that.

Success Leaves Clues

So let's define success as clearly as possible. We have an important task and a vocation from God. It's important to know precisely what we are seeking to do.

God is the Place. And we want our grandchildren to find Him. We want them to love Him. When they do, they will experience the best this life has to offer and also the best of the world to come. We will have laid the foundation for them to have a happy life.

So here is what success looks like:

- **Success Clue One:** Your grandchildren will attend Mass.
- **Success Clue Two:** Your grandchildren will develop a relationship with God and Jesus to give them the best lives imaginable, now and forever.

Now that we clearly know what we want, let's get to it. Let's craft your step-by-step guide for success.

Key Point
Success means your grandchildren will attend Mass and develop a relationship with God and Jesus.

Question to Consider
Envision the future of your grandchild. What does success look like for you and for him or her?

Action Step
Write the words of Success Clues One and Two on a card. Place that card where you will find it, see it, pray for it, and be inspired by it often.

Writing down your goals dramatically increases the likelihood that you will achieve them.

Prayer

O Lord, you are a good and loving Father. Help me to be a good and loving grandparent. Amen.

One Helpful Tool

My friend Richard, a father and grandfather, has been seeking this success throughout his years as the leader of his family. Not long ago, he wrote this letter to his children and grandchildren to be sure they know what matters most and to encourage them along the way.

Thanksgiving

A Letter to My Children and Grandchildren

Dear Kids,

Have you ever stopped to wonder, "What if it's all true?" What do I mean by that? Well, I'm talking about everything that Jesus said, revealed, or fulfilled! We have heard it, listened to it, even from time to time have thought about it. Over the last year in particular, I have been thinking about it a lot. It is a thought that will not leave me. I think that it is so "present in thought" to me because my Heavenly Father wants me to come to grips with it.

What does it really mean if it is ALL true? This much I know—if it is (and it is), then I can never be the same again. Not just one part of my life, not just an aspect here or there, but everything about me is forever to be changed. I can never be the same again.

Now whoa, wait a minute—that is a pretty strong statement. That's right, it is. I have come to understand that we have all spent our lives, at least those who even give God a moment in their thoughts and perhaps in their actions—hedging our bets. What do

I mean by that? Well, we want to believe everything that He says is true, but just to make sure, I am still going to make sure that I put myself first enough just to make sure I have a good time now and that "I" am going to be taken care of. I am not saying that we are not to be responsible for ourselves, particularly in providing for life's necessities. The last thing we are to do is be irresponsible. What I do mean is caring for "me" is not an end in itself but rather a launching pad to enable me to first and foremost care for those God has placed on the path before me.

If I spend my life preoccupied with me and my happiness, I will live life missing the deepest joy that God has for me.

When you stop, when you come to understand and deeply believe that this is only the beginning of our eternal walk with God our Father, everything is different. Different instantly, different forever. You are overwhelmed with the beautiful, deep, joyful, and penetrating peace that comes from knowing that you are home today and forever. Fear is gone forever. You are like a ship that travels along a coast of endless safe harbors. Storms may come but the harbor is always moments away.

I use the analogy of a ship because our new home with Christ, our new state of being, does not reside within four walls. On the contrary, it travels with us wherever we go. We have all been "dragged up from the deep" and have been set to sail into the wind, but from the safety of a ship that cannot be overcome by storm, famine, fear, anxiety, hunger, cold, loneliness, and despair. It is a ship ever on a new adventure but simultaneously anchoring in a safe harbor being constantly provisioned.

You have but one Captain: your Father, who is the Creator and Lover of all. He is not "like" a Father. He is your Father. He is more truly your Father than I can ever be. This is a defining difference, which is the foundation of all that is true. Your faith in the saving grace of Christ is a game changer. Live in full sonship and daughter-ship and receive the fullness of His love and constant care for you. He is your real Father every moment and beyond all time.

This new Captain under which you live and serve is like no other because He sends you forth in new freedom. A freedom that sets you free to do what you ought to do. To sail where you ought to sail. To explore and enjoy what you ought to explore and en-joy. It is your hands on the wheel, but He is ever present and at your side as long as you invite Him on the bridge. Draw courage, strength, and hope from Him. He is the farthest thing from a pup-peteer. It is true, all of it.

All of you are at different junctures in your lives, as are your spouses and your children. Where will your adventure take you and how will you go forth? Will you be like Peter, hedging your bets and looking at the storm- tossed waves? Or will you choose to see only the outstretched hand of Jesus. A hand that will never let you down. "What sort of man is this that even the winds and seas obey Him?" (Matthew 8:27).

In the end it is a choice, an individual choice to be made every day and every hour. But it is always the same question: "Is it true, every bit of it?"

Make the decision.

Love,
Your Dad and Grandpa

PART TWO:
SEVEN STEPS TO GREATNESS

START NOW

———

I am just one, but still I am one. I cannot do everything, but still I can do something. And because I cannot do everything, I will not refuse to do the something that I can do.
—Helen Keller

4. STEP ONE: **LOVE** LAVISHLY

*I knew my grandmother loved me
just by how she looked at me.*
—Jerry Ann Griffin

Nobody loves a child like a grandparent does. After all, a grandmother doesn't love you *if*. She loves you just because you are.

You Can't Live without It

When my two daughters were growing up, we lived about two hours away from my wife's parents. My girls loved their grandparents, Mama and Daddy Ray. They loved everything about them: being with them, eating at their home, playing in their yard, riding in their car, camping in horrific summer heat, going to buy new shoes. Everything.

Because Mama and Daddy Ray made our girls feel special. They loved them lavishly and unconditionally. When our daughters arrived at their grandparents' home, it was like the world stopped for a while. Mama had cakes prepared, and they ate. She had little gifts ready, and they celebrated a new toy or dress. Mama had all the time in the world, and she paid attention to each of my daughters. She listened attentively. She heard every detail of their lives, fourteen times. She and the girls slept together in the same bed, and still do whenever they are together. She lavished her love on them—so much so, when we pulled into the driveway of their home, Sarah-Ann and Griffin would leap out of the car almost before it had stopped. They would sprint through the yard, desperately lurching forward in hopes of being the first one to the porch and into the house. They did not stop to knock on the door. They barged in and yelled at the tops of their lungs, waiting to hear their grandmother, Mama, yell back in her melodious voice to reveal her location, "Yoooooo-hoooooo, I'm in the kitchen." And the girls would then run toward her, just to see her face and to be the first in her arms.

Nobody loves a child like a grandparent does. And in that love, the seeds of faith are born, the seeds that will lead to a full embrace from the loving arms of God as your grandchild grows up.

We know children begin their faith lives as they encounter the love of God early on in their lives. Love introduces kids to spirituality. And the two places children are most likely to encounter love are first with their mom and dad, and second with their grandma and grandpa. Secure family love lays the foundation for your granddaughter's faith. That love introduces your grandson to a God who loves him immeasurably. Faith begins with love.

Love your grandchildren well. Because when you do, you are pouring a foundation that will sustain them forever. You are preparing a place that will shelter them in the storm. Because that's what grandparents do.

Hug your grandson. Tell your granddaughter you love her every time you talk to or see her. May your grandchildren never doubt that they are loved first and foremost by you. Let your home be theirs, a place of refuge and security. Send gifts. Make video calls.

Text messages of love. Visit as often as you can. Sprinkle their lives with your love.

How you love your grandchildren will vary by where you live and your physical distance from them. How you love will also vary by their ages. In particular, there are three key windows of time as your grandchildren grow into adulthood. With each of those windows comes an important way of loving.

"Tony, what do you love about your grandparents?"

- They allow me to stay up late and play games with my whole family.
- They care about us.
- They make good food and always have treats that we like.
- They spend time with us.
- They talk to us on the phone.

Window One: The Basics of Love

Frederick II proved we cannot live without love. He discovered this truth accidentally in the thirteenth century. He wanted to test babies to discover what language they would speak if they never interacted with adults but only interacted with each other. Would they learn to communicate in Latin or in Greek? Or would they make up their own language, something completely unknown to adults? To find out, Frederick ordered a group of infants quarantined—separated from all adults other than a lone nurse who silently changed their diapers and provided some food each day. She interacted with the newborns on only the most basic level of need: food and cleanliness. She offered no kind touches, no words of affection, no smiles.

Frederick was shocked when the kids did not learn to communicate with each other. Instead, they died. They had received no love. Having no interaction with a loving caregiver meant the children received no love. No love literally meant death. Instead of learning what language they developed, Frederick discovered that without the love of a caring adult, the children could not survive. The absence of love equals death. Love is essential for our lives.

Loving your grandchild begins with making sure the basics are provided: food, safety, and loving care.

For the smallest of children, ages birth to two, love comes partly when their basic needs of food, water, and safety are consistently provided. Obviously, parents will take the lead role in providing these things, but you have an important role to play also.

When you help protect your grandchildren, when you help ensure their needs are consistently met, when you make your home a safe place for them, you are filling their lives with love. Love also comes when you give tender attention and loving care. In doing so, you saturate the children with love. And when you do so, you are placing them on the path to Jesus, who loves them most of all.

You can begin your grandchild's experience with love from day one. Hold her, rock her, sing to her. Feed him, protect him, smile at him. In so doing, you are introducing them to God. Love makes the difference between life and death.

Window Two: The Undivided Attention of Play

To grow up to be healthy, very young children do not need to know how to read, but they do need to know how to play.
—*Fred Rogers*

Children need attention. Attention communicates to a child that he matters, that he is valued. When adults are always busy and distracted, it causes children to feel marginal or even ignored. When we do not pay attention, children feel anything but loved.

As your grandchild begins to grow and develop, your love can take on new expressions. And your love can always be spelled the same way: T-I-M-E.

This usually means being fully present: being near and being available and attentive. Leo Tolstoy said, "There is only one time that is important. *Now!* It is the most important time because it is the only time when we have any power."

As the world speeds up with cell phones, families scurry from one activity to the next. With DVDs in the minivan, they eat dinner on the run.

Yet, no matter how lifestyles change, one constant remains: Love still means undivided attention. And undivided attention means time, and presence in the here and now. A grandparent is often in the best position to give that undivided attention.

Most of us adults are distracted. We have placed "undivided attention" on the endangered species list. But kids need attention. They crave it. Our multitasking, attachment to social media, and need for constant accessibility means we are always paying attention to lots of things at the same time. Or so we think. When you are paying attention to everything, you pay attention to nothing.

For a child younger than the age of eleven, the greatest way to show undivided attention and love is simply to play with him. Children communicate naturally through play. As one child expert says, "Birds fly, fish swim, and children play." It only makes sense. If you want to communicate with a child, use the medium with which she is most comfortable. That is play.

Too often, we adults think that spending time with a child means we have to be talking to them or teaching them a new skill. Actually, when we spend time with a child and play with them on their terms, we are teaching them love. We are teaching them that they matter. We are introducing them to carefree timelessness, to unmeasured fun, to unconditional love. What others might consider wasting time with your family is actually the highest investment you can make. Again, "I accept you as you are," not "I accept you *if* . . ."

Children are persons in their own right. They are not miniature adults; they are people. Your grandkids are unique and worthy of respect.

Play helps kids give their imaginations free rein and develop skills. It lets them learn what no one can teach them with words: to explore and get familiar with the world. They get physical contact and learn to get along with others and how to express their feelings. And when you enter into your grandchild's world simply by playing with them, you are entering on the friendliest, most loving terms of all: theirs.

When you play with a child, you bond with her. This is a huge part of the developmental process for children. Play is their world. Too often we expect kids to enter our adult world, when they are begging us to enter theirs instead. You love your grandson by entering his world and playing with him. Chasing balls, playing hide-and-seek, building forts and castles—time spent together, fully present, with your undivided attention. And the more frequently you do it, and for long, uninterrupted periods of time, the more you are establishing a loving bond that will last forever.

> "Jack, what do you love most about your grandparents?"
> - I like Mae Mae's snuggle time.
> - I like how Bumpa plays.

Best of all, as you play together, your granddaughter offers you the possibility of introducing her to the things and people that matter to you too. In that unfettered playtime, you get to include Jesus and maybe even a favorite saint or two. Dolls become friends and you can imaginatively act out stories such as God creating the world or the parable of the Good Samaritan. Books offer the chance to learn stories that will last a lifetime. You are entering your granddaughter's world on her own terms and communicating with her about what matters most to you.

You love your grandson, and play is his language. So why not communicate in the way he loves most?

Children's play is not mere sport. It is full of meaning and import.
—*Friedrich Froebel*

Window Three: The Undivided Attention of Listening

We all love it when someone actually listens to us. When someone sits, looks us in the eyes, and pays attention to our every word. When they give us their undivided attention. As your grandchild grows into adolescence and on into adulthood, active listening will be your best friend. This is especially true today, when undivided attention and true listening seem so rare. More often than not, the people around us are distracted and paying attention to their own things rather than to us. And when conversation does occur, it often comes through a device, where there is no eye contact, body language, or sincere reflections and affirmations being offered in response to what we say.

Just as free play with a younger child communicates attention and love, so does active listening as your grandchild moves into puberty, adolescence, and beyond.

As adolescence approaches, your communication will become more and more verbal as you are able to explore the emotions, beliefs, and deepest thoughts of your grandchild. Before eleven, your grandchild thinks more concretely. As they move toward adolescence, they begin to think more abstractly.

Here's the key. It just may be that the best way to love your grandson is to talk less and listen more, no matter what he wants to talk about. By listening to anything and everything, you will earn the right to listen to the important stuff when the time is right. Again, it's undivided attention. That endangered species that is so important communicates love.

By age eleven, your grandchild will most likely be fully immersed in the world of cell phones, social media, and constant communication. But her emotional needs will be the same as yours were when you were eleven—only now they will be harder to fulfill because of all the distractions. Here is where you come in.

Early studies are discovering that increased time on social media and constant access to phones and computers actually lead to higher levels of isolation, loneliness, and depression. This is especially true for girls.

The adolescent years can be lonely and hard for both boys and girls. You have the opportunity to be a great friend to your grandchild through those years. What is a friend? A wise man once said, "A friend is the one who comes in when the whole world has gone out."

As the grandparent, you probably will have no say in the decision about when your grandchild gains access to a cell phone. However, you can begin to use that phone to communicate love, whether you live nearby or across the globe. One of the gifts of technology is that it can narrow the distance between families that are scattered around the country—when it is used intentionally and proactively.

Undivided attention communicates love. The gift of time comes along as you listen attentively, whether by phone, by FaceTime or Skype, or in person. By simply being available and listening, you provide the antidote for busyness. In a world where no one ever seems to be fully present with anyone else anymore, you can give the generous gift of undivided attention: active listening and sustained eye contact. Time and attention are the supreme gift of love.

Listening, time, and attention communicate love because they are a sacrifice. There is no love without sacrifice. When you're giving your grandson undivided attention, you are saying no to other things and opportunities so you can be fully with him. You give him your deepest yes. You are saying, "I love you. You matter. More than anything else around me right now."

Those who met Pope John Paul II felt this same kind of undivided attention. He had the gift of making you feel like you were the only thing on his mind for that moment you were together. That is a sign of holiness. And it is a sign of love. Because with God, we always have His undivided attention.

Unconditional, unmeasured, unadulterated love. It's a good thing. And too much of a good thing can be wonderful.

"Elizabeth, what do you love most about your grandparents?"
- Their openness to talk
- Their willingness to offer other opinions
- They love you.
- They always make you feel welcome.
- They are smart.
- How generous MawMaw is. With everything. She always has time.

Extraordinary Sacrifices

Think of someone you deeply love. When you do, it is usually easy to think of a time when they made a sacrifice for you.

- Canceled a trip to stay with you when you were sick
- Left a meeting so they could talk to you

- Used their vacation time to come visit you rather than going somewhere else
- Stayed home to help you with your homework rather than going out to a movie or a ball game
- Walked slowly with you at your pace rather than rushing on ahead to be with the crowd
- Sent you money in a card rather than buying something they really wanted for themselves
- Worked an extra job just to pay for your music lessons

Love is not about compromise; love is about sacrifice. Providing food and security requires sacrifice. Giving undivided attention requires sacrifice. Active listening requires sacrifice.

And sometimes love requires a lot.

When Clarence's father abandoned his family, Clarence and his brother were sent to live with their grandfather, Myers Anderson. When they arrived, Myers said, "The damn vacation is over." Clarence's grandfather was tough, even severe at times. He loved excellence, and he demanded it from the people around him. He maintained very strict rules for everyone in his house. And the boys eventually grew to call him Daddy.

Children in Myers' house were expected to rise early, work hard, and keep their opinions to themselves. No whining, no excuses, no back talk. If they kept to the program, they just might end up in what Daddy called a "coat-and-tie job."

Myers made the raising of Clarence and his brother his life's work. He sacrificed everything else to pour into these two boys. Clarence and his brother had plenty to eat and their own beds—neither of which they'd ever had before. Chores and schoolwork took priority over everything else at the Anderson household, and Myers never wanted to hear any excuses. "Old Man 'Can't' is dead—I helped bury him," he would tell his grandsons.

Clarence says, "He never praised us, just as he never hugged us." Myers was severe and not always in a healthy way. Beatings with a belt or switch were part of his approach to rearing boys. When Myers bought a new truck for his business, he took out the heater. He didn't want the warmth to make the boys lazy.

Myers, a convert, sent his grandsons to Catholic schools and saw that they became altar boys. As Clarence reached high school, Myers paid for him to attend a Catholic boarding school, where Clarence was one of only two black students.

When Clarence graduated, he studied to become a priest but dropped out, and when he did, his grandfather kicked him out of the house.

The trauma from that experience, and the separation from his grandfather for many years, still causes Clarence deep pain. The two reunited briefly when his step-grandmother was in the hospital; they had a healing conversation and embraced at the end. But his grandfather died the next month of a stroke before Clarence had another chance to see him.

Nevertheless, Myers Anderson redirected the entire course of Clarence's life. Clarence knew he could trust his grandfather, even when he did not like him. That trust, and the sacrifices Myers had made for Clarence's education and formation, created an unwavering self-confidence in Clarence—enough that Supreme Court Justice Clarence Thomas could write in his autobiography, "Neither then nor at any other time did it occur to me that I could not do the work of a Supreme Court justice." And for that self-confidence, there is one person to thank: his grandfather.

"What I am," Justice Thomas writes, "is what he made me."

Time, play, presence, attention, listening, sacrifices—over time, these all show love, even when we are not perfect. From this all else springs forth. We value and follow those we trust and love. If you want to help lead someone to the Place, they will have to trust you first. To trust you, they will first need to know you love them. And they will see that in your sacrifice.

You must see what great love the Father has lavished on us by letting us be called God's children—which is what we are!
— 1 John 3:1, New Jerusalem Bible

STEP ONE: LOVE lavishly. Love your grandchildren well. They are learning God's love as it is embodied in you.

========

Key Point
No one loves like a grandparent.

Question to Consider
What have you done to be sure your grandchildren experience your love for them?

Action Step
FaceTime (or spend time in person) with your grandchild today.

Prayer
Lord, teach me to love like you love: lavishly.

One Helpful Tool
Prayer of a Grandmother

Lord,
I have counted each day waiting
I have whispered new names each
   night
I have held this grandchild forever

I have dreamed dreams
Beyond my imagining
That come to life in the
Tiny fingers that wind around my
   thumb

Whatever this grandchild is
And will become
May he know the wisdom of Your
Temple days
May he lift the wounded with Your
   healing way
May his heart be humble should he
   stray

When your mother let you go
Did she walk the dusty roads forever
   in her heart
Following You with love

Or did she learn to trust
Even when You walked that hill
And spread your arms
For me
And all humanity?

Help me place my life, my flesh, my
   grandchild
Into Your care, Your arms
Mind him for me
Mind him well

Then one day, Lord
He can tell his child
Of you and of love
As well.

(Adapted from Fr. Liam Lawton, *Hope Prayer*)

5. STEP TWO: **PRAY** PASSIONATELY

Pray without ceasing.

—1 Thessalonians 5:17, NAB

My son-in-law Killian (Allen and Matthew's father) is in the Navy. Because of that, their family lives hundreds of miles away from Anita and me. The distance motivates us to create as many ways as possible to give Allen and Matthew undivided attention, love, and the gift of time. We make that drive a lot, but we also use FaceTime with them. Each morning, we get Allen's face on our phones, usually as he eats breakfast, and we just talk. We laugh with Matthew, we listen, we learn. Most of all, we are with them, albeit imperfectly.

Even when Allen was just learning to talk, we listened attentively to his grunts, groans, and cries, just to be fully present. We want him to know that he matters. We love him. And we want all of our grandsons to have our undivided attention as an expression of that love. That's how we build the relationship.

Build Your Relationship

In a deeper way, just imagine how much God delights in spending time with you. If FaceTime with our oldest grandson, Allen, has become the highlight of our earthly day, just imagine how much your heavenly Father delights in seeing your face and hearing your voice. He's the Father who made you. Who breathed His life into your body. Who knows the number of hairs on your head. Who feeds you with His own Body and Blood. Who gives His Son, Jesus, to you. He loves you immeasurably and desires to spend time with you most of all. He wants to build the relationship with you.

That is what prayer is: spending time with God. Building a relationship with the one who loves us most of all.

St. Francis de Sales compared our prayer time to a holy ladder. When we take time away from the world to spend time with God, it is like the heavens open and a ladder descends. Jesus takes a step or two down toward us. We take a step or two up toward Him. And He looks deeply into our faces and listens to us with love.

When we do, we build the most important relationship of all.

One Christian pastor put it this way:

I have a seven-year-old granddaughter . . . named Madeline. She is blonde, skinny, and tall for her age. . . .

What I want Madeline to know is that the best thing about prayer is the relationship itself. Whether or not she gets what she asks for, I want her to keep asking. I want her to pester God the same way she pesters her mother, thinking of twelve different ways to plead her case. I want her to long for God the same way she longs for her father, holding fast to him even when his chair is empty.

When she complains that none of this does any good, I am going to ask her to tell me the difference between how she feels while she is praying versus how she feels when she thinks about giving up. If I am lucky, she is going to tell me that she feels more alive when she is praying. . . .

That's right! We feel most alive when we pray. Because that's when we are connected to the one who is life itself. The best thing about prayer is the relationship. Build your relationship.

It All Begins Here

To help your grandchildren get to the Place, your first step will be to begin with prayer. It just makes sense. If you want to help your grandchildren get to the Place, you have to visit and know it yourself. In prayer, you do just that. You go to the Place, you remain there awhile, and you get to know it well. And then you actually have something to give.

In our research at Dynamic Catholic, we have found that the single most important spiritual habit is prayer. It generates the greatest spiritual results and harvest of any habit we can have. On the one hand, that doesn't surprise you, does it? I mean, Jesus regularly took time away, often early in the morning or late at night, and went off to a quiet place to pray.

On the other hand, our research found that most of us do not have a daily routine of prayer. Oh sure, we pray. We pray a little here. And we pray a little there. But we quickly get distracted, or fall out of the habit, or just turn to prayer when we need something in a hurry. "Oh Lord, please help me find a parking space. I've got a lot to do today."

Please hear the results of our research one more time: The greatest determinant of the health of your soul is prayer. It's the number one habit. Nothing else comes even close. If you want to be a-better-version-of-yourself, it will begin with prayer. All else flows from this. Prayer will define the quality of life for your soul.

Ten minutes a day can make all the difference in the world. The more time you spend in the classroom of silence, the more clearly you will hear the voice of God in your life. Having a daily routine of prayer means having a time, a place, and a structure. You will pray and you will tend to do it each day at the same time, in the same place, and in a regular way that works for you—spending time in silence, listening for the voice and the nudging of God; sitting in His presence, giving Him your full attention even when you are saying nothing at all. In a world where the average American spends more than eight hours a day in front of a screen (TV, computer, smartphone, etc.), stepping away from the noise into the silence can be revolutionary. In fact, it's a game changer. Clarity emerges from silence.

Without prayer, you are operating on your own power. You're an eight-cylinder car, but you are only using two. You are still moving, just not very well.

With prayer, each day over time, your relationship with God will build, and your life will begin to change. Prayer works on your soul much like waves come in day after day and slowly change the coastline. It's consistent, steady, powerful.

Habit experts have shown time and again that one habit lived well begins to change everything in your life. They usually call this the keystone, or gateway, habit. For example, the decision to run a 10K race will lead to the decision to run each day to get ready. That daily habit of running may soon lead to the decision to quit smoking to be able to breathe and run better. That habit may gradually cause you to eat differently and to drink differently. You are caring for your body so that it can run each day, to get ready for the race. That habit may also force you to rethink how you sleep. Again, you are slowly adjusting to the habit of running each day.

Day by day, bit by bit, week by week, your keystone habit has created other habits and decisions that have revolutionized your physical life. After a few months, you not only are running each day, but
you are slimmer, healthier, and experiencing more energy than you
have in years. The keystone habit opened the way for that.

God invites you to make prayer your keystone habit. A daily
routine of prayer is the ultimate game changer. As you begin to
pray consistently, you will notice other parts of your life opening
up in healthy ways you never anticipated. That time with God will
spill over into multiple areas of your day. You might have more
peace, experience more patience, find relationships deepening, or
live with more confidence. As your prayer life goes, so goes your
spiritual life.

And as your prayer life goes, so goes your *life* life.

The Power of Laser Focus

As you build your relationship with God, you will naturally want
to lift other people into His presence. He will love you, and you
will love Him. And because of that love, you will want to place
other people into that same loving presence. You will want to ask
for His hand and His help for people in special ways.

Pray *for* your grandchildren. Of course, you can pray *with* them,
and we will discuss that more in the next two steps. But right now,
I invite you to pray *for* them. Pray for each grandchild by name,
each day. Take your time. Be specific.

Doing this will give part of your prayer time a sharp focus. And
nothing changes things like focused prayer. You are praying each
day for each grandchild and his or her circumstances, by name.
That's laser focus.

Remember, you are on a mission. You want to pass the torch to
your grandchildren. Praying with focus will invite the power of

God to invade your mission. And you and they will no longer be operating on just two cylinders.

For Robert, a grandparent in Michigan, that means praying a rosary each day, with one decade for each of the families of his five children, and within each decade, a bead or two for each grandchild and parent. This is a perfect example of focused prayer, consistently applied each day.

Our Dynamic Catholic team has designed a simple, straightforward way to help you develop a daily routine of prayer. We call it the Prayer Process.

The Prayer Process is a simple way to have a conversation with God each day during your quiet time. Through prayer God helps us to become the-best-version-of-ourselves, to grow in virtue, and to live holy lives.

It goes like this:

- Step One. GRATITUDE: Begin by thanking God for whoever and whatever you are most grateful for today. You may want to begin with thanking Him for His immeasurable love in your life.
- Step Two. AWARENESS: Think about yesterday. Talk to God about the times when you were and were not the-best-version-of-yourself.
- Step Three. SIGNIFICANT MOMENT: Ask God what He is trying to say to you today. Talk to Him about that.
- Step Four. PEACE: Ask God to forgive you for anything you have done wrong and to fill your heart with peace.
- Step Five. FREEDOM: Talk to God about some way He is inviting you to change and grow.
- Step Six. OTHERS: Pray for the other people in your life by asking God to guide them and watch over them. In

particular, pray for each grandchild. Name them one by one. Simply lift them into the presence of our loving Father and ask for His mercy to rain down in their lives.

• Step Seven. Pray the Our Father.

You are taking very simple steps forward. First you are building your relationship with God by stepping onto that holy ladder. Then you are lifting other people, particularly your grandchildren, into that same relationship of love.

And slowly, over time, your focused prayers will not only change them but will also begin to change you, just like the waves crashing into the coastline.

Become the Prayer Champion for Your Family

Just imagine what your family would look like if you made it your one goal to pray each day for their faith and their lives. Do you think your regular, consistent prayer might make a difference? How might your family be changed because you resolved to leave a prayer legacy?

Mama, our daughters' grandmother, decided early on to do just that. She has been praying for her grandchildren each day since the first pregnancy was announced. She keeps a little prayer journal, with a section of it devoted to praying with focus for her grandchildren each day. She has a written verse of Scripture by each grandchild's name, chosen individually, a theme verse she uses to pray for them. It's nothing elaborate or complicated—just consistent prayer for grandchildren and their own burgeoning families, day after day, year after year, like waves crashing onto the coast. She is the prayer champion for our family.

And her grandchildren know that. They walk into the world each day knowing that their grandmother has been and will be praying for them each step of the way. Each of those grand-children has made both great choices and poor choices. They are human beings, like every single one of us. But they have the daily assurance that someone is praying for them with great love. And that makes all the difference in the world.

What would happen if you decided to become your family's prayer champion? What might your life and theirs look like if you combined your great love from step one with His great love here in step two to pray with focus each day? Prayer champions are often the difference between a child who grows up to be a practicing Catholic and one who doesn't.

Wherever Matthew Kelly and I go in our work at Dynamic Catholic, we encounter parents and grandparents who are heartbroken because their children or grandchildren have left the Church. And then there are people like Kathleen and Allen Lund. When Matthew was having dinner with them, he discovered that his hosts have six children and twenty-two grandchildren, all practicing Catholics. So Matthew wondered who were the prayer champions in the past and the present of this family. This is Kathleen's father's story.

On the afternoon of January 24, 1945, American soldier Eddy Baranski was executed at the Nazi concentration camp in Mauthausen after having been brutally tortured for days. He was a son, a husband, and a father. Eddy's father never spoke his son's name again for the rest of his life. His mother prayed for her boy every day for as long as she lived. His young wife, Madeline, had a vision of him smiling at her, at what she would later learn was the very moment of his death. And his daughter, Kathleen, who was just two years old when her daddy went off to fight Hitler, spent her life fatherless, unable to remember his voice, his touch, or his smell.

Fifty years later, Kathleen's daughter participated in a study abroad program in Austria. While visiting her in Austria, Kathleen decided to go to Mauthausen. There she stood in the basement where her father had been tortured and shot in the head. She stood there as if waiting for something—some feeling, some message—but there was nothing.

Returning home, Kathleen began inquiring more about her father. She spoke with relatives, wrote to the National Archives, to museums in Europe, and to the United States Army. Slowly, the story of a father she had never known began to emerge.

In 1945, Werner Muller, a German citizen, dictated an extraordinary document to an Austrian lieutenant. The multilingual Werner had worked as an interpreter under Heinrich Himmler. In October 1944, Muller was ordered to Mauthausen, where his job was to translate the interrogations of Allied prisoners. He described the next three months as a living hell. Muller remembered one prisoner above all: Eddy Baranski.

He described Baranski praying as a group of Nazi officers tortured him. The commandant asked the interpreter what he was saying, and when Muller revealed that he was praying the officers all burst into laughter. They then offered Baranski a drink by placing water on a table, but the torture had left him incapable of raising his arms or hands, and they would not raise the water to his mouth. Muller described this as the worst afternoon of his life.

Little by little, the story of the father she had lost so early in life was coming together for Kathleen. A couple of years later, she visited Piest, Slovakia, where her father had been captured, and the house where he was living at the time of his arrest. There she met Maria Lakotova, who wept when she remembered Eddy Baranski. Maria shared with Kathleen that Eddy used to sing lullabies to her at night when she was a young child in that house.

"Your father would hold me. I would sit on his knees and he would sing to me," Maria told Kathleen. "But I know he was not singing to me; he was singing to you, his little girl so far away."

Kathleen never knew it, but her father was singing to her—and he was praying for her. Eddy Baranski was a prayer champion. Every family needs at least one. Today Allen and Kathleen are continuing the legacy by praying for their children and grandchildren each day.

Every family needs a prayer champion. What would happen if your family's champion was you? Great things would happen.

STEP TWO: PRAY passionately for your grandchildren. By name. Each day.

Key Point
Without prayer, you and I are merely operating on our own strength and vision. With it, we are operating on the power of God.

Question to Consider
What does your prayer life look like?

Action Step
Spend ten minutes today using the Prayer Process.
Pray with laser focus for your grandchild(ren).

Prayer
Lord, teach me to pray. Better yet, teach me to listen. Amen.

One Helpful Tool
Prayer for a Grandson

Lord,
Why is it that at the most confusing
 time of our lives
We have to learn the most
We have to carry so much within
We must learn to listen
We must listen to learn

All is decision
All is choice
All is question

Help my grandchild to find friends
Who will accept him
Help him to be strong
When difficult choices come
Help him to live with values that You
 value

When he is anxious
When he is hurting
When he is confused
When he is lazy
When he is troubled
When he is fearful
When he is rejected
When he is ridiculed
When he is moody
When he is misunderstood

Be with him, Lord

When he is happy
When he celebrates

When he wins
When he falls in love
When he passes with flying colors
When he finishes the assignment
When he finds his place
When he belongs

Be with him, Lord

Teach him understanding
Team him compassion
Teach him empathy
Teach him respect
Teach him graciousness
Teach him forgiveness
Teach him courage
That others will find in him
What he longs to be

On each new day
Bless those who love him
Bless those who teach him
Bless those who befriend him
Bless those who accept him

Bless his family and friends
All who know him

May all that he has learned
Be not in vain
For if he has never lost
He will not search again.
Amen.

(Adapted from Fr. Liam Lawton, *Hope Prayer*)

6. STEP THREE: **DREAM** DEEPLY

It is Jesus that you seek when you dream of happiness;
He is waiting for you when nothing else you find satisfies
you; He ... provoked you with that thirst for fullness that
will not let you settle for compromise ...
—St. John Paul II

Dreams are powerful. Dreams change lives. Dreams change the
world. And each of us has them.

Dream On

God has given us human beings incredible gifts. The ability
to dream is one that is astounding. We have the ability to look
into the future, imagine something bigger and better, and then
come back into the present and bring about that future we've
dreamed of.

God placed a dream on Abraham's heart, a dream of a people
who would belong to Him alone. God stirred a dream inside King
David to build a great temple for His glory. St. Joseph had a dream
and learned he was to follow through with his marriage to Mary,

the Blessed Mother, and receive the gift of the child Jesus. That dream changed everything.

In fact, St. Joseph's dream opened the path for dreams to inspire and propel the saints. St. Catherine of Siena dreamed of a re-united and holy Church. St. Teresa of Calcutta dreamed of a world where each person has dignity regardless of caste or location. St. Francis of Assisi dreamed of a renewed Church. And St. John Paul II dreamed of freedom from the bondage and oppression of Communism.

What would the world be like without someone like Martin Luther King Jr., who dreamed of a better future? How many people could look into the future and see that Ichijirou Araya would climb Mount Fuji at one hundred years old? He was probably the only one who could see that dream! Or how many people could look out at a flat stretch of land in New York City and envision the Empire State Building? What would the world be like without people who can look into the future and see things that no one else can see?

The passion of dreams is contagious.

Dreams are God's gift to us. They offer new possibilities. We all have dreams. God places them in us and stirs them. Some dreams are small, like the dream of a healthy relationship or a fruitful career. Some are much larger, like the dream of curing cancer. Some dreams are God-size and bold, like the dream of peace in war-torn countries.

Kids dream naturally. And in those dreams children have as they grow and mature, we find the seeds of the spiritual life, and something bigger. In those dreams, children find their purpose for life and their passion for living.

When you help a child to dream, you help him or her listen for the voice of God. Kids will dream on their own; when you join them in that journey, you nurture their faith and inspire their future.

And when you belong to Christ, you discover God has big dreams for your life. God wants you to look just like Jesus: patient, joyful, gentle; peaceful, loving, kind; faithful, generous, self-controlled. That is the-best-version-of-yourself.

That dream alone will transform your grandchild's life. She will live up to the high expectations and hopes of God rather than down to the low expectations of the world and the culture. Her body will have value and dignity because it is God's temple. Her mind will dream big and think clearly because it is the mind of Christ. Her life will have meaning and direction because she seeks God and His vision in all that she does.

Our dreams are the visions that shape our lives. Do you know what your dreams are? Have you stopped dreaming? Sometimes we do. When we stop dreaming, we slowly begin to disengage from our relationships and from life itself.

The most fascinating people we all know are those individuals who are engaged in life and with what their dreams are. These people are interesting to us.

Dreams are what should get you out of bed in the morning.

Dreaming will animate you and help you live a life uncommon. It will help you live God's dream for you and your family. And your grandchildren's dreams will change their lives forever.

The Power of Questions

How do you help your grandchild to dream? Ask questions.

Questions make us grow. They stretch us and prod us to explore things we might never otherwise think about or discuss.

In a dream workshop with the Dynamic Catholic staff, each staff member was asked to answer a few short questions, one of which was "How many dreams do you currently have?" One of our staff members said that she had answered that question with a zero. She did not have any dreams—she said she had always been a very content person and was happy with her life. She didn't need anything more and felt like having dreams was almost selfish. She said that over the course of the exercise she realized it was in fact the opposite—that it was selfish *not* to dream. She had discovered that God gave us the ability to dream so we can grow and become the-best-version-of-ourselves. We serve Him and one another through the very gift of dreaming and working toward those dreams. This young woman had one hundred dreams written by the end of the exercise.

God gave you the ability to dream! It's the most powerful ability He gave to us besides free will—and we all have it. We all have the ability—and the responsibility—to dream. What are you doing with that ability? Dreaming with your grandchild is one of the most beautiful forms of intimacy and an incredible exercise in continually learning about one another.

And remember you are never too old to dream. Sharing your own dreams and reflections will stimulate even more questions from your grandchild. Those questions plant the seeds of dreams and stir their hope and faith.

The Power of Dreaming Together

Once you ask questions, listen. Few people listen to children. Even fewer listen to them over and over again. Children love to talk. Even more, they love to be heard. We all do.

Remember the first step in your plan: Love lavishly. We feel loved when someone really pays attention and listens intently to us.

You have the privilege of listening deeply to your grandson and his dreams for his life, his world, his future. When you give him that listening ear and look him in the eye as he talks, you are communicating your deepest level of love. He knows you love him. He knows he matters. And when he knows that, he will dream bigger and bolder. Because you will have given him the confidence to dream. And your conversation will guide his dreams and help him find the voice of God. You have that power, simply by doing what no one else will do: listening attentively time and time again.

Recall how Kyle Maynard's Grandma Betty spent hours and hours with him. She listened as he struggled with the physical challenges that came with his birth. She listened as he dreamed of a life that made sense, one where he had value, where he used what God had given him for some kind of purpose.

Grandma Betty listened and guided those dreams to help Kyle discover that his life did indeed have meaning. Her attentiveness showed him that he mattered and had value, which helped Kyle to find the courageous dreams of mountain climbing and becoming a world-class athlete. He then leveraged that to become a motivational speaker helping others overcome any kind of disability. Dreams come from God. And they are nurtured by a listening grandparent.

Few people listen. Science's best guess is that we miss 75 percent of what people say to us and around us. We listen to only a quarter of what people say. Isn't that unbelievable? You can change that with good questions, helpful reflections, and paying attention.

We all need someone to hold us accountable for our dreams. Together, as a team, you and your grandchild can hold each other accountable for achieving your dreams. This can be a joint journey for life. Now, that is a gift!

There is something incredibly fulfilling about helping someone else achieve a dream. It is a form of intimacy that is rare but extraordinary. In helping each other live our dreams, we become personally invested in each other—one of the fundamentals of a healthy relationship. You have a personal interest in watching that other person succeed and in knowing that you are helping him or her grow and stretch.

We are more engaged with our grandchild when we dream together. Nothing animates a person like chasing down a dream. The passion and energy that are the telltale signs of this animation cannot be confined to one area of our lives—they overflow into all aspects of our lives. Two individuals chasing down dreams individually and together are going to have an extraordinary relationship—it will be more dynamic, more animated, more interesting, with a level of personal investment that goes beyond living out the day-to-day together. Dreaming together is a recipe for a wonderful relationship.

Not all of your dreams will come to fruition. Your dreams will change, you will seek new ones, life will knock you down, and unexpected challenges will come your way. You will have to let go of some dreams in order to say yes to others. It's been said that God answers prayers in one of three ways: yes, maybe later, or I have a better idea.

When life knocks you down, or something for which you can't prepare happens, it's the two of you—together—who will work to get back on track or find new dreams. How you handle and navigate these changes and challenges will make all the difference in your relationship. Support each other, encourage each other, talk about your dreams, and be open to new ones. Always be working toward at least one of your dreams. Celebrate when you achieve it. Never stop dreaming together.

Ask the Most Important Question

Adults ask children the same question all the time: What do you want to do when you grow up?

It's the wrong question.

Instead we should be asking: *Who* does *God* want you to *be?*

Notice three key differences in this question from the popular phrasing of "What do you want to do when you grow up?"

1. WHO, not what
2. GOD, not you or someone else
3. BE, not do

First, WHO you become matters far more than what you may do in any certain area of your life. We are made for greatness, for humility, for generosity, for love, for joy, for faithfulness. That is WHO we are and want to be—people of character, people of holiness. What we do is merely an expression of the person we are and are becoming.

Second, when we consider what GOD wants for our lives, the question takes on a whole different angle. It is not so much what your grandchild wants at any given time as it is helping them to see that GOD has big dreams for their life. Listen for those. "You belong to God. What does He want? That matters far more than what you or any person wants for your life. He made you. He loves you. He designed you for greatness. How does *He* see your life?" Now, *that* is a question.

Third, who you *are* matters far more than what you *do*. Your life consists of more than merely how you make a living. BE a saint. BE the-best-version-of-yourself. BE who God wants you to be. And only then will your life have the passion and purpose you seek.

WHO does GOD want you to BE? That's the single most important question of all. Ask that over and over with your grandson as he grows up and you will have placed the central idea in his mind for all time. He will return to that question over and over again as he matures. You will be pointing his life toward purpose. He will be heading toward an eternity that belongs to God rather than merely focusing on a job or a career as if that is all life has to offer.

Remember what I asked you early on: If you had a choice between your grandchild having a great career and your grandchild having a great faith, which would you choose? God is teaching you something in your answer to that question.

When your grandchild sees the future and explores it with God's help, then she or he can begin to make it happen.

Ask the right question. Listen and guide. Over and over again. That is how you will light the fire. Dream on.

STEP THREE: DREAM deeply *with* your grandchild. Ask the right question.

―――――

Key Point
In the end, there is only one question that really matters: Who does God want you to be?

Question to Consider
How well do you really listen?

Action Step
Get a dream book and begin the following dream exercise by writing down three dreams today.

Prayer
Lord, teach me to ask the most important question. Amen.

One Helpful Tool
Here is a sample dream exercise. The beauty is you can do it with

your grandchild. Sharing your dreams will inspire theirs and build intimacy and a lifelong journey. You will be with them the rest of their lives as they dream.

Dreams can manifest themselves in hundreds of different ways and can take any number of years to achieve. They often have a financial component, but many dreams worth pursuing don't cost anything at all. Dreams come in all shapes and sizes. And they get to be your dreams, not the dreams of other people you see, or what the media tells you. They are *your* dreams.

Here is an exercise to help you get your dream list started. Achieving dreams is a habit, and one that can start today!

The rules for dreaming are only this:

- Create a dream book/journal and write in it often.
- Date your dreams twice: when you write them down, and then again when you achieve them.
- Look back on your dream book often. You'll find that the dreams you have already accomplished will give you the courage to chase your unaccomplished dreams.
- Never stop dreaming with your grandchild.
- Move boldly in the direction of your dreams. To warm up, start with just a few questions:
    - If you could vacation anywhere, where would it be?
    - If you could be front row at any concert, what would it be?
    - If you received a million dollars tomorrow, what would you do with it?
    - If you could start a charity, what type would it be?

Sometimes it's helpful to think about dreams in categories. Spend some time thinking about the following categories and what dreams you have that fall under each one. There is a question to help prompt you, but we have also included a list of sample answers for each category below. Do this yourself first, and then go through and do it with your grandchild.

- *Adventure:* If you could travel to any three places in the next ten years, where would you go?
- *Creative:* What hobby or sport would you like to grow and develop?
- *Physical:* What aspect of your physical health and wellness would you like to improve?
- *Legacy:* What ministry, cause, or charity would you like to support or increase your support toward?
- *Emotional:* What one relationship would you like to improve or grow?
- *Psychological:* If you could suspend fear, what activity would you try?
- *Professional:* What's your dream job?
- *Intellectual:* If you could speak an additional language, what would you speak?
- *Spiritual:* What's your dream for how you might develop a greater sense of inner peace? Who does God want you to be?
- *Character:* What character qualities do you notice in other people that you would like to expand in your own life?

SAMPLE ANSWERS:
Adventure:
- visit the Great Wall of China
- visit the works of Monet in museums in Paris
- climb a 14,000-foot mountain

Creative:
- write a book
- learn to play guitar
- take a painting course

Physical:
- look and feel healthy
- run a marathon
- lose weight

Legacy:
- raise my children to have a healthy sense of who they are
- volunteer and donate at my favorite ministry
- do my part to help the environment

Emotional:
- own my own home
- be in a great relationship
- really try to listen more

Psychological:
- strengthen my willpower
- overcome my fear of heights
- face my addiction

Professional:
- get a promotion
- build a dynamic team or department
- develop a new product

Intellectual:
- go back to school
- learn another language
- read more

Spiritual:
- develop greater inner peace
- learn to enjoy uncertainty
- become a person of great love

Character:

- develop patience
- do what I say I will do
- earn respect by being completely trustworthy

Many of the dreams listed here are also dreams you can work toward together, as a grandparent and grandchild. Begin a wonderful journey of fulfilling dreams together.

7. STEP FOUR: **MODEL** MASTERFULLY

---

*Don't worry that children never listen to you; worry that
they are always watching you.*

—Robert Fulghum

Harold and Ruth Knapke embraced each other and never let go.
More importantly, they embraced the faith and never let go.

The Whole Town Knew It

Harold and Ruth met in the third grade. No one would have
guessed they would go on to enjoy a lifelong romantic relationship
that included sixty-five years of marriage. The Knapkes went to
Mass together, prayed together, played cards together, and danced
together each Saturday night in the den of their home. Undivided
attention and affection saturated their relationship. And so did
their Catholic faith.

Harold saw himself as Ruth's protector during their sixty-five
years of marriage. He worked as a teacher, a principal, and a coach.
Ruth worked as a school secretary after being a stay-at-home
mom. As their health declined, the couple moved into a nursing

home, where they still shared the same room so they could care for each other. The caregiver would get Ruth tucked in each night and then Harold would go in, pray, and bless his wife with holy water and give her a kiss. It was part of their daily routine, a habit.

The Knapkes welcomed six children into their Ohio family, followed by fourteen grandchildren and then eight great-grandchildren. Each of them discovered the Catholic faith right before the Knapkes' very eyes. You couldn't miss it. Harold and Ruth embodied it every day. It was just part of who they were.

When Ruth's health took a turn for the worse, everyone knew death was not far off. Harold, whose health had been poor for some time, held on as long as he could, hoping to protect Ruth all the way to the end. Finally, early on a Sunday morning, he died. Ruth followed him in death that afternoon, just eleven hours later, in the room they shared. They fulfilled their wish of crossing the river together into the next life. And they made that transition only nine days shy of their sixty-sixth wedding anniversary. One of their daughters said, "I think he decided, 'No she's not going without me.'"

What happened next inspired their entire town. The Knapke family celebrated Harold and Ruth's sixty-five-year union with a joint funeral Mass at their home parish. The granddaughters gently carried Ruth's casket; the grandsons lovingly carried Harold's. The Knapke children, grandchildren, and great-grandchildren laid Harold and Ruth to rest together in the cemetery, fully surrounded by their Catholic faith. It was just who Harold and Ruth were. And their grandchildren saw it every day.

Harold and Ruth Knapke modeled love. And they modeled faith.

Walk the Walk

"You can't give what you don't have."

The Church developed this expression early on to capture the truth of the formation of priests. In Latin: *Nemo potest dare quod non habet.*

What it means is that if the priest has a shallow faith, that is all he has to share. If he has a poorly formed faith, he can offer only that to the people he serves. But if he has a robust, vibrant faith, then he really has something to offer the people.

After all, you can't give what you don't have. It's a basic truth. No one is exempt. There are no shortcuts.

It is true for you and me too. If we want to pass on our faith, we can only pass on what we have. We can't give what we don't have. There are no shortcuts. No one is exempt. Not even grandparents.

When your grandkids think of you, what do they think of? Do they know you are Catholic? Can they see it?

Or think about it this way: If you were put on trial for being Catholic, would there be enough evidence to convict you? It's one thing to talk the talk; it's another to walk the walk. As Flannery O'Connor wrote, "About the only way we know whether we believe or not is by what we do."

Simple ways to walk the walk include simply being positive rather than negative. Build your grandchildren up. Don't say negative things about their parents if at all possible. Say good things about others. Try your best not to talk about people or gossip in front of your grandchildren.

Fill your language with God words: Use God, Jesus, and Holy Spirit in your talking. Add in phrases like, "let's remember the Golden Rule," "bless you," and "count our blessings."

Walking the walk occurs in the small things every day. And no one did that better than Lawrence. He was born to a poor family in Lorraine, France. Lawrence received no formal education, although he turned out to be far wiser than most humans. He became a soldier, then a household servant for a group of monks in Paris when his military service had ended.

The monks were set apart exclusively to pray, to worship God, and to seek the heart of the Lord. To help them live out their mission, Lawrence spent each day in the kitchen, sweeping, scrubbing, cleaning, and cooking. He saw himself as the "servant of the servants of God." His was a life of humble, menial service—cooking, cleaning, and mending shoes.

From the day he entered the monastery, Lawrence lived the rest of his life doing the menial tasks that many of us dread, put off as long as we can, or hire someone else to do. The odd thing was, Lawrence took great pleasure and joy in those menial tasks. Because he had a habit—of living every moment in the presence of God.

Lawrence made a deliberate effort to worship God in every task he did. Every pot he scrubbed, he scrubbed as an act of worship to God. Every pan he rinsed, he rinsed as an act of worship to God. Every floor he mopped, he mopped as an act of worship to God.

Lawrence gave himself over entirely each day to a life of simple worship and devotion to Jesus.

He found ways to drive out of his mind anything capable of interrupting his thoughts of God. He developed a habit of worshipping God all day long, by returning to Him in the midst of every task. His goal? He said it was "to become completely God's. To give my all for God's all." He lived as if there were nothing in the world except him and God.

By reminding himself over and over, eventually he made worship his habit. Worship was not something he had to remember to do but something that just flowed naturally in everything he thought, said, and did. What he found was that by repeating the acts, he developed a holy habit, taking everything he did and turning it into worship.

And people came from all around to ask him questions and to seek his wisdom on life. Even the monks sought out advice and insight from the cook and scrubber of their kitchen. Lawrence radiated a simple peace, and everyone found that peace attractive. You can only give what you have. Clearly, Lawrence had a lot to give.

Lawrence became known as "the lord of pots and pans." He wrote private notes, only discovered after his death. A leader of the monks then assembled those notes and put them into a book, *The Practice of the Presence of God,* so that others could read how Lawrence transformed every mundane moment into glorious worship and praise of God.

Your grandchild is watching everything you do. And she is probably going to imitate it too! Do you walk the walk? What faith do you have to give to your grandchild?

What if you were to follow the example of Brother Lawrence? How might you live out your faith in everything you do?

Pray, "I belong completely to you," as you fold clothes, as you drive to work, and as you go through your day. In the middle of a task or a project, say to God, "Shape this for your glory, O Lord. I belong to you." As you meet people, silently say to yourself, "Bless this person, O Lord." When you rise in the morning, say, "Here I am, Lord, ready to do your will."

If you want to pass on your faith, you have to have a faith worth passing on. You can't give what you don't have. What do you have that you would like to pass on or share? A deep faith that shows up in everything you do? A regular prayer life? A life of study? Generous giving? Kind service to people in need? An enthusiastic desire for God and His dreams for you and your family?

Be honest. How are you doing? What do you have to share?

There is not in the world a kind of life more sweet and delightful, than that of a continual conversation with God; those only can comprehend it who practice and experience it.
—Brother Lawrence

Let Them Catch You in the Act

We imitate what we know. We have a tendency to re-create what we are exposed to at an early age. Dr. Martin Luther King Jr.'s grandfather and father served as pastors, so it makes sense that he chose that path too. Dale Earnhardt Jr.'s grandfather and father raced cars, so it makes sense that he followed in their footsteps. Jacques Cousteau's grandson loves the oceans and makes films just like his grandfather did. Children often embrace the professions and vocations of their parents and grandparents.

We also imitate the habits and lifestyles we observe as children. For example, children of alcoholics have a much higher likelihood of creating alcoholic families than kids who grow up in nonalcoholic settings. Children of divorce are more likely to get divorced than kids raised in families that remain intact. And children who grow up immersed in the Catholic faith in their families have the greatest probability of being practicing Catholics as adults. We imitate what we know.

Rebecca spent a lot of time with her grandmother, Cecelia. She called her "Gran."

Rebecca's mom worked on weekends for most of the years Rebecca and her three sisters were growing up, so Gran took the four girls to church each Saturday. She would pick them up at 4:30, go to 5:00 Mass with them, and then take them home. Once a month, Gran would pick up the girls early and take them to confession before Mass. She wanted them to have the faith. She wanted to light the fire.

Rebecca so loved the order and structure of her grandmother's house that she began to spend each Saturday night there, while her sisters went home. After Mass, Rebecca and Gran would eat dinner at home or perhaps at a restaurant with one of Gran's friends. After dinner, they would play a game, do a crossword puzzle, and watch the news until the sports report came on. They would kneel on the hardwood floor and say their prayers. Then they would go to bed. On Sunday morning, the two would wake up and head to Gran's garden to tend the vegetables.

Gran loved the faith. She kept a rosary nearby at all times—in her chair, in her lap, on the nightstand by the bed. She went to Mass each weekend and wanted to ensure her grandchildren did too. Slowly, Rebecca came to love the faith and going to Mass just like Gran did. Children imitate what they see.

Gran worked hard. Her husband had passed away when her own children were small, and she had little money to get things repaired, so she fixed things herself. Gran loved to cook, and she prepared meals for any crowd at any time. Rebecca learned to love to cook too. Gran gardened to raise a lot of her own food. She grew tomatoes, radishes, peas, cucumbers, and rhubarb. She and Rebecca tore down the garden each year together and burned all the remnants, a yearly ritual that remains Rebecca's favorite memory of their special time together. Gran worked hard, and Rebecca learned to do the same—so much so that she earned a PhD. in neuroscience, during which time she got married and birthed her first three children.

Gran fostered family rituals and traditions. One of these traditions was Christmas cookie day, when she and the grandchildren would devote a full day to preparing hundreds of cookies to share with friends, family, and the parish staff. Others included the weekly meal at her home for all her children and grandchildren and the annual Thanksgiving and Christmas Eve feasts she prepared even as the crowd grew ever larger with grandchildren and their new spouses, and then the great-grandchildren too. Rebecca loved those meals. She sat in the same place every time, next to her grandmother, with her back to the wall farthest from the kitchen, but still the one always chosen to go and fetch whatever Gran needed at any given moment. Rebecca loved to serve her grandmother and loved serving next to her most of all. Being next to Gran was her special place, and Gran's house was Rebecca's most favorite place of all.

As Gran aged, Rebecca and her sisters would mow the lawn and care for her house. When Gran died at age ninety, Rebecca was twenty-four. Knowing the end was near, she spent the last two nights with Gran, soaking in every opportunity to be near her. "She was just important to me. She was my best friend."

We tend to re-create what we know. Rebecca still holds the annual Christmas cookie day. She works hard. And she takes her children to Mass every weekend, just like she learned from Gran.

Your grandchildren are going to imitate someone. Let that someone be you! More important, let what they imitate be your own practice of the faith.

In fact, let them catch you in the act. Do not stop praying when your grandchildren walk into the room. Let them catch you praying. Feel free to take them along as you ladle chili at the homeless shelter in town. Let them catch you serving. Invite your grandchildren to hold the check with you as you place it in the offering plate or into the envelope to mail to your parish. Let them catch you giving.

When you do these things, you become the model for a master-apprentice relationship. You are modeling behavior to be imitated. You are walking, not just talking. And they will walk with you because they are serving like apprentices. They will observe your habits and begin to follow suit. Your grandkids will learn the faith slowly but surely over time in the little things, until it becomes part of the air they breathe.

The Catholic faith is caught more than taught. Take your grand-children with you on the journey. Rejoice when they walk in on you; invite them to accompany you; let them catch the faith from you. They will imitate what they know.

Lois did that very thing for her grandson, Timothy. The proof came when St. Paul wrote to him, "I am reminded of your sincere faith, a faith that lived first in your grandmother Lois and your mother Eunice and now, I am sure, lives in you" (2 Timothy 1:5). Lois did her work well. Her grandson grew up to be St. Timothy.

All the research shows that faith is best passed through practice. A child sees a person they love practicing the faith and begins to follow suit. That loving parent or grandparent lives out the spiritual life, takes the child along, and guides them along the path.

That is how the foundation gets laid and how the torch gets passed.

Your Story

The more your grandchildren catch you in the act, the more they will begin to ask questions. They will ask you *what* you are doing. Then they will ask *why* you are doing what you are doing.

I look forward to the times I can take my grandsons to Mass. In each portion of the Mass, I speak the words over them: the Gloria, the Creed, the mystery of faith. I hold one or lean over one and say the words. I want each grandson to hear those words even before he can speak them himself, before he can fully know what they mean. I want the words of faith to be as natural and comfortable for him as they are for me. I want them to saturate his life and guide it as he learns to walk, run, talk, read, and believe for himself. I want him to catch the faith—from me.

I look forward to his questions like "What does 'Hail Mary' mean?" "What are those beads?" "Incarnate? What is that?" "Who is Gloria?"

Then, "Why do you come to Mass each Sunday, Grandpa?" "Why are we buying these backpacks to give to other kids?"

These moments provide opportunities for great conversation. In these conversations with your grandchild you will pass the torch.

Catholics have a great story. We feed and educate more children, clothe more people, and house more families than any other group on earth each day. That is *our* story.

But to answer your grandchildren's questions, remember to tell *your* story. Share with your granddaughter what *you* love most about being Catholic. Tell your grandson *how* the faith came to be so important to you. Laugh as you offer him a memory or two about your first trip to reconciliation or the time you fell asleep in Mass when you were a teenager. Shed a tear as you share how your prayer life helped you hold it all together when your best friend died or when you lost a job. Tell your story. That is what will inspire your grandchild most of all. No need to polish it up—just be honest and real. Your faith is who you are. And your grandchild will love knowing everything about that.

Our Catholic story is important to know. And it's fun to tell. But your story matters more, because it is *your* story.

Live. Show. Teach.

Research shows that kids most frequently learn the faith from the people who love them most, and that you share the faith and pass the torch when you model these three simple ideas: Live. Show. Teach. In that order.

Live the faith.

Show them the path.

Teach them the way.

And that is why the next chapter is so very crucial.

STEP FOUR: MODEL masterfully. Walk the walk, and let your grandchildren catch you in the act.

———————

Key Points
You can't give what you don't have.
Faith is caught more than taught.

Question to Consider
If you were on trial for being a Catholic, would there be enough evidence to convict you?

Action Step
Write your faith story. In one page, sketch out how you came to love the Catholic faith, what you do now, and why it is so important to you. Writing it down will help you be ready to share that story with your grandchildren when the time is right.

Prayer
Lord, I yearn to follow you most of all. Amen.

One Helpful Tool
Use a Mass journal each week when you attend Mass. Write down during Mass the one thing God is telling you or saying to you about becoming the-best-version-of-yourself. You not only will focus more during Mass, but you are modeling that behavior for your grandchild. You can do this together.

Get a free Mass journal at dynamiccatholic.com/massjournal.

8. STEP FIVE: **BUILD** HABITS BOLDLY

Train up a child in the way he should go, and when he is old he will not depart from it.

—Proverbs 22:6

St. John of the Cross said it first: God's purpose is to make your soul great.

How to Have a Great Soul

Have you ever had a holy moment? Of course you have.

A moment when you knew you were doing exactly what God wanted you to be doing, when you knew you were being exactly who God made you to be. That's a holy moment.

Holy moments come in all shapes and sizes. There are small moments, like a moment in prayer when you are simply sitting in the classroom of silence and are overwhelmed by the presence of God all around you. You can just feel His love right then and there.

There are medium-size moments, like a challenging conversation with someone you need to forgive—and you do it. You actually forgive that person. The conversation ends with a warm embrace. You just know that you are slowly becoming who God wants you to be.

And then there are large moments, like the one my daughter had. For her sixteenth birthday, she went to a Caribbean island—not to enjoy the blue waters or deep-sea fishing, but instead to visit a land of severe poverty. Our family celebrated Griffin's sixteenth birthday there while serving as part of a mission team that includes funding a soup kitchen in a parish in Soufrière, the poorest fishing village on Saint Lucia, untouched by the tourism at the other end of the island. The kitchen serves the destitute in this remote village and is staffed completely by volunteers.

The pastor invited our team to walk the streets of Soufrière, distributing meals to those physically unable to make it to the soup kitchen. Griffin and I walked alongside David, a retired government worker who has chosen to live in the poor village of his childhood rather than enjoy the comforts of his pension in a more luxurious and developed area of the island. David distributes food each day, checking on the infirm, the dying, and the disabled in this little village. His presence brings cheer and comfort to people living on the edge each day. Eyes brighten, smiles appear, and countenances change as David walks the street.

Griffin and I accompanied him on his circuit, serving the villagers of Soufrière, who are among the poorest people in the Caribbean. Surrounded by natural beauty looking out on the sea, while looking into the eyes of a person dying from neglect and hunger, startled both me and my sixteen-year-old daughter. The contrast could not have been greater.

As we accompanied David, our team was on a tight schedule. We had several places that we planned to be that day, so we had only about an hour to assist with the work of the soup kitchen. Toward the end of our time with David, we stopped by a "home" constructed of trash: paper towel tubes, empty food cans, construction scraps. This home belonged to an elderly woman, Isabella, who ate at the soup kitchen each day and then took three or four meals with her to give to people who lived near her but who could not walk to the kitchen. When we stopped by, she was not home, and David discovered that she had been hospitalized the night before. David immediately realized her illness meant the other people counting on her would not receive meals.

He began heading back to the soup kitchen to retrieve meals for those others. I pointed out to him that our American team did not have time to do that right now. David kept walking. I reminded him again of our tight schedule, that we needed to be elsewhere on the island in just a few minutes, and that these other people's meals would simply have to be arranged in a different way. David kept walking. You get the picture—uptight American self-importantly placing timelines and his own schedule before the basic needs of the poor. Not very inspiring at all.

By the time I realized how absurd my behavior must have appeared, we had already arrived back at the soup kitchen. We gathered additional meals and worked our way back to David's neighborhood to share them with the people counting on Isabella for their food that day. One such man was Kenneth, who lived in a lean-to that really cannot even be called a hut. Made of plywood in a square, his "house" was probably six feet by six feet. There was barely room for a cot. There was one hole cut in the plywood for a window. Kenneth weighed no more than eighty pounds, his skin hanging on his bones like a sweater on a coat hanger. He looked to be about seventy years old, though with his physical condition and poverty, it was hard to tell.

So around midday, my daughter and I knocked on the "door" of the plywood house to share a meal with Kenneth. With what little strength he possessed, he mustered a word of gratitude and began to eat his simple meal of a piece of bread and a bowl of soup. We told him that we felt honored to bring his meal, that God loved him, and that we did too. We had a brief prayer with Kenneth and then headed back to our bus to meet the rest of our mission team.

Two things still stay with me from that visit. First, the immense simple holiness of David, a man who has given the golden years of his life over to serving the poor in his little home village with dignity and grace each day. David has no ego, simply a heart full of love and a desire to serve God and His children. He embodies the words of St. Teresa of Calcutta: "I belong to Jesus; He must have the right to use me without consulting me."

Second, on her sixteenth birthday, my daughter Griffin was serving among the poorest of God's people, gently offering food and grace in His name. No sweet-sixteen bash for her. No extravagant self-indulgence. Just my daughter, discovering the holiness and peace that often exist serving among the poor. It is a peace that often is missing in the busy American suburbs where we live.

As we climbed back onto the bus that day, I leaned over and whispered in Griffin's ear, "I am really proud of you. Happy birthday. I love you." For her sixteenth birthday, Griffin received a true holy moment.

How does God make your soul great? With holy moments, small, medium, and large. Holy moments place you in the pathway of God. The more holy moments you experience, the closer you get to Him. And the closer you get to God, the more you become the great soul He intends you to be.

How do you discover holy moments? With habits. Our lives change when our habits change.

Your soul is like a sailboat journeying toward God. But what makes a sailboat move? Not the power of the sailor, but the power of the wind. The power for the movement comes from outside the boat and its sailor. In the same way, the power for your journey comes not from you or from your soul but from the power of God. The Holy Spirit propels your soul forward.

An excellent sailor knows how to position herself in front of that wind, knows how to be in the right place to harness that power. An excellent sailor has the skills and the habits to do this. She knows how to do the same things every time, so that when the wind arrives, she is ready. She knows how to clean the boat, measure the depth of the water, tie the knots, position the sails, and navigate. She can capture the wind and make her way toward her destination.

In the same way, your spiritual skills and habits help you capture the wind, the Spirit of God. The more you are able to harness the power of God in your life, the more holy moments you will experience. The more holy moments you experience, the more your soul will move toward Him, and the greater you will become.

The Four Life-Changing Habits

If you want your soul to become great, seek to experience holy moments as often as you possibly can. If you want your grandchild's soul to become great, help him experience holy moments.

If you want more holy moments, how can you increase their frequency? With habits. By doing the right things over and over, you will be more likely to be ready when the Spirit blows like the wind in your life.

We are what we do. Our lives change when our habits change.

An athlete becomes an Olympic medalist not in a single day, but in the daily training habits successfully performed slowly but surely each day for years. A best-selling novelist achieves greatness not through one grand brilliant day or month of writing, but through practicing, writing, editing, revising, being critiqued, and rewriting day after day for years. A world-class investor builds wealth not in one big lucky deal of the century, but through saving and investing with discipline day after day for years. Greatness takes time. And it takes habits.

Our lives change when our habits change. Habits determine greatness. And you were made for greatness.

Much of my life has been spent with families asking me to help fix problems with their younger children, teenagers, or grandchildren. As we talk, it often becomes clear that the family formed unhealthy habits along the way, and those habits have produced unexpected and undesired results in the children shaped by them.

For example, one family organized their entire life around one of their children's passion for baseball. The parents were surprised when over time, their other children grew resentful of spending every weekend on the road for one sibling's baseball games. "Do we have to go? Why is it always about him?" And they were startled when they realized their children had little or no faith life because every weekend had been spent focused on baseball rather than on God, the parish, and the family. Who had time for faith when all the family's time and money revolved around baseball? Worst of all, the family's baseball player child turned out to be self-centered and one-dimensional. That just makes sense, because his family had focused every bit of their time, money, and attention on him and his passion for baseball, to the exclusion of everything else. He learned that it was all about him.

A lifetime of bad habits cannot be fixed in a single counseling session or with wishful thinking. Habits form us, and they form families, for good and for bad. Unhealthy habits produce unhealthy people and unhealthy families. Great habits produce great souls.

When Jack's grandson made his first Communion, Jack sat down with him and read the inspiring words of John 6:25–59, in which Jesus shares that He is the bread of life. When we eat His flesh and drink His blood, we receive eternal life. Jack wanted to be sure his grandson knew the beauty of the moment when he first received the Body and Blood. Nearly a decade later, when the grandson turned sixteen on the other side of the country from where his grandfather lives, he wrote his grandfather, Jack, a letter. In it, he shared that he had just finished reading John 6:25–59 on his birthday, and had been reading it every year on his birthday since his grandfather had spent the time to do it with him at his first Communion. Through a grandfather's simple action, a lifelong habit had been formed.

Dynamic Catholic takes habits seriously. Our team spends enormous amounts of time and energy studying and researching them. In fact, our work to reenergize the Church in America began with a groundbreaking study to find the life-changing habits of the most spiritually engaged Catholics across the country.

We invested three years of work and money in that research. We conducted 2,978 interviews with priests and the engaged Catholics they pointed us to. And we came to discover the four life-changing habits that lead to spiritual greatness. These four habits are proven to be the most likely to lead to the holy moments God wants for you.

We call them the four signs of a dynamic Catholic.

- **Prayer**: Having a daily routine of prayer. Ten minutes of conversation with God each day. This is the crucial, number one habit. All else flows from this.
- **Study**: The average dynamic Catholic reads for fourteen minutes a day, or five pages a day. He reads a good Catholic

book, studies the Bible, or explores the faith in order to
learn to think like God thinks rather than the way the world
thinks.

- **Generosity**: Being radically generous with your love, your
  money, and your time. Our research found a direct trans-
  formational link between the generous giving of money and
  spiritual vitality.

- **Evangelization**: Finding at least one way each month to
  share the genius of Catholicism with another person, whether
  with words, passing along a book or CD, or another act.

Very simply, our research found that these four habits lead to the
greatness you want and seek. These four life-changing habits will
reinvigorate your soul, your family, and your parish.

So, the obvious conclusion is this: **if you want your grandchild to attain greatness, help him or her develop these four
life-changing habits.** Because our lives change when our habits
change. We are what we do. Habits determine greatness.

The Power of Experience

How do you develop these habits in your grandchild?

First, by practicing them yourself, as we discovered in the previous chapter. You can't give what you don't have.

Second, by sharing with your grandchildren experiences that
embody one or more of these four habits.

Too often in the Church, we think that passing on the faith comes
from the passing on of information. "If we can just get them good
information and catechize them, then we will be in good shape." It's
true that catechesis is important, but remember that faith is more
caught than taught. The heart matters just as much as the head.

Learning to play golf does not occur primarily in a classroom, and neither does learning to embrace and live the faith. It occurs in little experiences and habits that happen regularly over time.

And just as Jesus said to love God and to love your neighbor, becoming a person of faith is every bit as much about loving (heart) as it is about knowing (head). And how do you learn to love? With heart experiences.

We learn by doing just as much as we learn by formal instruction. And this is never more true than when it comes to passing on the beauty of the Catholic faith to your grandchild. You inform minds, but you inspire hearts.

The experiences you share with your grandchild will populate her spiritual memory for the rest of her life. Never underestimate the life-changing power of little holy moments that happen with you over time. Those will form the spiritual language and identity of your granddaughter even when she is a grandparent herself.

Some of these experiences you will simply share as you practice the four life-changing habits together, like Rebecca and Gran did. Others you will instill in a deep way through the traditions you help build in your family. Time and again, the research shows that family traditions are crucial for forming rhythms and behaviors in children that will track all the way into adulthood. For example, the simple tradition of eating dinner together as a family has been proven to produce stronger families and more socially connected children. These traditions become the structures for your grandchild's life, much like the framing becomes the structure for the way your house is built. All else hangs on it.

In summary, these four life-changing habits are *proven* to lead to those holy moments. Practice these four habits with your grandchild every chance you get and you will be building the habits that will last a lifetime. You are the guide, with your grandchild following you on this journey.

The next section provides fifty-one ways to build these lifetime habits.

Fifty-One Simple Ways to Build Habits Boldly

God loves each of us as if there were only one of us.
—St. Augustine

Grandparents come in different shapes and sizes, and so do grandchildren. Some grandparents live far away from their grandchildren; some live nearby. Sometimes grandchildren's parents are not as interested in the faith as the grandparents are. Sometimes divorce has created challenges for the family and for interacting with grandchildren.

You will know your situation best of all. This list is designed to provide a variety of options and possibilities that can be applied based on your situation. Some of these will work well for you and your circumstances; others will not. Choose those that do. After all, this is *your* plan.

PRAY

1. **Sing "Jesus Loves Me"** to your infant, toddler, and preschool grandson. Rock him as you do so, if you live nearby. As he develops, let him sing the words with you. The repetition will embed those words deep in his memory and soul. You're building his friendship with Jesus, the Lord of life. And you can do this in person or long-distance by phone or FaceTime.

2. **Teach her the Our Father/Lord's Prayer.** Thomas Merton, the famous monk and writer, learned the Our Father from his grandmother. Repeat the words with your grandchild in person and when you are in Mass together. Give it

as a gift, with the words on a plaque or bookmark. Recite it by phone or in a card.

3. **Pray together at meals and invite your grandchild to take a turn in the rotation by praying aloud.** By doing this at home and in restaurants, you teach your grandchild that prayer is normal, helpful, and important.

4. **Pray together by asking your granddaughter about her day before she goes to bed.** Ask her if there are things or people she would like to pray for, and then pray for them. In fact, feel free to pray spontaneously with your grandchildren whenever the opportunity presents itself.

5. When your grandchild or your family faces struggles or adversity, **pray together when you gather as a family.** Include your grandson. Let him see and hear you talking to God, in times of fear and suffering.

6. **BUILD A TRADITION: Use an Advent calendar each year in the season leading up to Christmas.** The calendar will have accompanying pieces of material to support it with Bible readings and prayers. Again, this can be done in person or as a long-distance gift. Build the memory of each Advent being a special experience with you as the grandparent, and build the tradition of prayer inhabiting your grandchild's Advent through the use of the Advent calendar.

7. **Walk the Camino together.** Pilgrimages have power. Can you imagine the memory and learning that would occur if you and your grandchild walked part or all of the Camino together, breathing in prayer with every step?

8. As Catholics we have lots of built-in opportunities to leave special mementos to inspire prayer. **Give your grandchild the gift** of a rosary at first Communion. A Bible at confirmation. A photo of you all together for a baptism. An album

of memories from Christmas celebrations each year. These special presents will stir moments of prayer each time your grandchild looks at them and remembers your faith together.

9. **You can also provide special gifts** that will stay with your grandchild always. A crucifix necklace as a birthday gift. The gift of a ring for a wedding. Or the framed pictures of Jesus with children that hung in my daughters' bedrooms for years and that now hang in my grandsons' bedrooms. Again, these will stimulate prayer consistently over time.

10. **BUILD A TRADITION: Pray over the Christmas cards your family receives.** Collect all the cards from December and then pray for the family who sent you each card at a meal in the coming year. Invite your grandchild to do this with you in person or long-distance. Our family likes to start praying over them on Ash Wednesday as a way to prepare our hearts for Easter. It makes a great connection between Christmas and Easter.

11. **Get a dream book and use it with your grandchild.** Check in regularly on how these dreams are coming. If you live at a distance, routinely check in via a text or call.

12. **Send a regular prayer card.** Handwritten notes and cards are an endangered species in our electronic world, but they will hold great power. Write your granddaughter notes of blessing and she will likely hang on to some or all of them, displaying them on her refrigerator, leaving them on her nightstand, or using them as bookmarks. These are all regular reminders of your prayer for her and an invitation to pray herself.

13. **Take your grandchildren to Mass when you travel together.** Build in the awareness of the universal Catholic Church, people praying together all over the world.

STUDY

14. **Sing often.** Sing well. Use a song you particularly love from your family's worship and prayer life. Sing it as an offering of worship to Christ Jesus. Memorize it and sing it with your grandson. Shape his soul and mind with music. You will build a lasting memory deep within him.

15. **Identify key decision moments in your grandchild's and family's lives.** Baptisms, first Communions, confirmations, and other special moments like that. Capitalize on those moments by having personal conversations with your granddaughter about Jesus and your own friendship with Him. Invite her at those moments to make Jesus her own friend.

16. **Use free resources from Dynamic Catholic** like *Blessed* (animation and workbooks for first reconciliation and first Communion), *Decision Point* (videos and workbooks for confirmation), and *Rediscover the Rosary* together (www.Dynamic Catholic.com). Many families and grandparents use these resources regularly for faith enrichment and formation rather than just at the time of preparation for the sacrament. If you live at a distance, you can easily do the videos together.

17. Make the most of the teaching moments that constantly occur when you are together to **discuss the right thing to do with your grandchild.** Whether it is in the store and you receive too much change and give it back to the cashier, or at the dinner table discussing your grandchild's day and a difficult decision he faced, seize these moments and have a good conversation about what it means to be a friend of Jesus.

18. **Gift a book.** Perhaps give one each Christmas as a part of your gift, and give one for summer each year. You will be surprised what can happen when twice a year you give the

gift of a good, engaging, age-appropriate book about the faith. You might even offer to pay your granddaughter a small amount of money if she reads the book and writes a short summary of what she read. My own grandmother did this for me to inspire me to read and to study.

19. **Purchase a kids' Bible.** Read it at night with your grandchild. Learn the stories together and discuss them. Excellent children's Bibles are readily available. Find one that is age appropriate for your grandchild, and spend a few minutes before bedtime each night reading it aloud. You are discovering the wonderful words of Scripture alongside your grandchild, so your own gaps are being filled even as you are building his foundation.

20. **Make memory verses a part of your family life.** I highly recommend memorizing a Scripture verse together as a family every two weeks and then reciting it together aloud. This practice will build the bonds in your family and place the words of the Bible deep in the memory of your granddaughter.

21. **Discuss the messages from Mass each Sunday.** Each weekend, after Mass, use the time in the car, over a meal, or by text or phone to share what you heard and learned. Focus the conversation on what your grandson specifically discovered that day about God and himself, which can be a springboard for a discussion about how to live that out in the coming week. This tradition of the family conversation about one thing each family member felt God was saying to them at Mass will pay dividends in your family for generations to come.

22. **Use a Mass journal.** Instill the regular discipline of going to Mass and listening for the one thing God is saying to you

this week. Dynamic Catholic makes these available for kids; teenagers can easily use the adult version. Then you can discuss together as mentioned in number 21.

23. **BUILD A TRADITION: Celebrate the patron saints of grandparents and set aside November 21 each year for the Presentation of Mary,** an ancient tradition in the Church in which we remember how Mary's parents, Sts. Anna and Joachim, took her to the temple to present her for a life consecrated to God. Anna and Joachim offered Mary to God in the Temple when she was three years old, to carry out a promise they made to God when they were still childless. From the beginning of Mary's life, she was dedicated to God. Find a way to celebrate and discuss this each year with your grandchildren so that it becomes a part of your family's faith and you remember the crucial role of grandparents in the life of Jesus.

24. **BUILD A TRADITION:** Read aloud the Christmas story in Luke 2:1–20 at Christmas each year when you are together in person.

25. **BUILD A TRADITION: Decorate the Christmas tree and set out your family's nativity set at the same time each year.** Do it with your grandchildren in person when possible. Place the consistent memory of this special family time deep inside them.

26. **Use Resurrection eggs** when your grandchild is small. These little teaching tools help you share the Passion of Christ so that a young child can begin to grasp the story and the signficance of Holy Week and Easter.

27. **Take a pilgrimage to Italy or the Holy Land** with your grandson. Expose him to the holiest places of our Catholic faith. Experience the presence of God together. These

powerful experiences will remain with your grandson for the rest of his life.

28. If you live at a distance from your grandchildren, **arrange to come and be a part of their parish youth retreats, confirmation retreats, or service projects.** Your sacrifice of time and travel will signal to your grandchildren that they are valuable and that the faith matters. You can chaperone or be a volunteer. The parish will be grateful for your help too.

Focus on these messages with your grandchild:

29. **Ages seven through eleven (forgiveness, justice, and displaying love toward others)**
   "I can choose what is right."
   "I need Jesus' help."
   "I am a part of God's big family."
   "Jesus died to save me from sin because He loves me."
   "The Eucharist is special. I get to receive Jesus."

30. **Ages three through six (compassion, friendship, and knowing right from wrong)**
   "I like to listen to Bible stories."
   "I know Jesus feels sad when I do something wrong."
   "I know who God is and what He is like."
   "I can talk to God whenever and wherever I want."
   "I know how I can love and serve God today."

31. **Ages zero through two (comfort, love, and trust)**
   "God created all things."
   "God the Father cares for me and provides for me."
   "Jesus, God's Son, loves me."

GIVE

32. **Be a generous person and your grandchild will become one also.** Involve your granddaughter in the giving decisions of your family so that she understands what you give and why. Let her fill out your pledge cards at the parish. Teach her how giving your income to God's ministries sets you free from selfishness and materialism. Show her how to give to help other people.

33. **Look for events that allow your family to share compassion.** Make sandwiches and chili to give to a homeless shelter, bring peanut butter for a local food pantry, or purchase a few extra school supplies at the beginning of the year to share with children who don't have them.

34. **Practice thankfulness to God.** Ask your grandchild, "What three things are you thankful for today?" Being grateful for all that God gives helps us to grow a thankful, generous heart. It makes a great discussion starter to help you keep connected with your grandchild's life, decisions, and priorities.

35. **Visit a nursing home resident regularly with your grandchild.** Take cards. Bake cookies. Give flowers. Just sit and share time with a lonely resident.

36. **Spend a Saturday or Sunday at a mission for homeless men, women, and children.** Prepare breakfast and lunch. Worship with people who live in boxes, beneath tarps, or in the woods. Serve them with God's grace. Their dignity and gratitude will expose your grandchild to the heart of God.

37. **Sell lemonade** and give the money to a ministry your grandchild is interested in.

38. **Let your grandchild place your offering in the plate at Mass.** At a parish in Minnesota, the priest holds the

children's offering basket at the front of the church. As the ushers gather the offering from everyone else at Mass, the priest, like a good grandfather, invites the kids to come forward and place their offering in the basket at the front. When he does, bedlam follows! Children sprint out of the pews and down the aisle to get to the priest with their gifts. One child dives with his dollar bill toward the priest. Another runs at breakneck speed all the way up front and then back to her seat. It's like the Olympics of giving. Enthusiasm explodes. And the priest is teaching the children the habit of generosity.

39. **Read *Life's Greatest Lesson* with your grandchild.** This short book tells the story of a grandmother and her relationship with her grandson as he grows up. The story will inspire you and equip your grandchild with tools for faith and generosity.

40. **Pay part or all of your grandchild's tuition** for Catholic school or college. Give the marvelous gift of a faith-based, Catholic education.

41. **BUILD A TRADITION: Go on a mission trip as a family each year.** Serve people and churches in areas of need such as Venezuela, Costa Rica, or St. Lucia. Exposing your grandson to the poverty of the world will shape his heart for the rest of his life. He will view his own life with purpose and grace rather than with selfishness and conceit. He will see his possessions as gifts from God to be shared rather than as entitlements to be hoarded. Doing this regularly will not only shape your grandson's soul with generosity, but will build special memories of time with you that he will carry forever. If you live at a distance, use your vacation time to make that possible. Your sacrifice will model generosity and inspire your grandchild.

EVANGELIZE

42. **Share your faith.** Talk to your grandchild about what you learned from a homily or from your own prayer time with God. Discuss important holy moments you have had in your life, particularly as a child or teenager. Share about someone for whom you are praying. Let your grandchild see you reading your Bible, praying, or choosing to be kind. Faith is caught more than taught.

43. When your granddaughter expresses a desire to talk about Jesus, **seize the moment.** Listen attentively. Give her your undivided attention.

44. **Share a good Catholic book or CD** with your grandson and help him to share it with one of his friends. For your younger grandchildren, giving Eliot Morris' CD of children's music can be powerful.

45. **Invite one of your grandchild's friends** to attend parish activities (like children's choir or vacation Bible school or first reconciliation/first Communion) with your grandchild. If you live nearby, help make that possible by serving as driver or volunteer.

46. **Pray specifically by name with your grandson for one of his friends** who does not participate in the parish. Ask him if he has any friends he would like you to pray for. Pray that God would stir that child's or his family's hearts with the flames of faith.

47. **Teach your granddaughter to do something special for a friend's birthday.** One example might be to have a Mass said for that friend's intentions. First, you model this by having a Mass said each year on your granddaughter's birthday and sending her a special card to share it. Then, teach her to do the same for three of her friends.

48. **Give the gift of a faith-filled movie**, like *The Passion of the Christ, A Man for All Seasons, Chariots of Fire,* or *Schindler's List.* The options can be extensive. Films can share the faith in powerful ways not possible otherwise. Introduce your grandchild to the faith with the gift of a trip to the theater together, a DVD, or shared time watching a film on Netflix.

49. **Use social media.** Be engaged with your grandchildren as much as they will allow you to. Choose one form of social media and occasionally post words of encouragement or even thanks to God for something great happening in your grandson's life. First, you are participating in his life where he spends the most time (social media). Second, you are modeling encouragement and faith with simple positive, faithful words.

50. **Collect stories and pass them on to your grandchildren.** Jesus told stories because people remember them. Collect stories, tell them, write them down. Stories from your own life, from your family, from the faith; stories about your grandchildren's times with you or of watching them do great or funny things; good family stories of faith; good family stories of failures or lessons learned. Most of all, pass on good family stories of love. Stories about you, about your marriage, about your parents and grandparents; stories about the Church, your faith, and great priests; stories about how a saint changed your life. Populate your family with stories of greatness and love, and those stories will change the future.

51. **BUILD A TRADITION: Invite one of your grandchild's friends to attend Easter Mass with you each year.** Build the habit of inviting others to the faith. Create a tradition of including people at Easter, the most important day of the Catholic year.

STEP FIVE: BUILD boldly the four life-changing habits of spiritual greatness in your grandchild.

═══════════

Key Point

Our lives change when our habits change. Habits determine greatness.

Question to Consider

What traditions does your family have?

Action Step

Pray *with* your grandchild (not just for them or in front of them). Build the habit. Begin now.

Prayer

Lord, teach me to be a good guide. Amen.

One Helpful Tool

Use the fifty-one easy ways listed in the previous pages to begin now. Pick just one and do it well. No need to bite off too much. Habits change in small, digestible pieces.

9. STEP SIX: **CONNECT** CREATIVELY

Associate yourself with people of good quality, for
it is better to be alone than in bad company.
—Booker T. Washington

"Like attracts like."

Plato said that, and he's right. You and I tend to become like the people we live with, hang around, or are close friends with. Over time, we develop goals, habits, and a purpose similar to those of the people we spend the most time with. We even begin to look like the people we hang around. In fact, one study in *The New England Journal of Medicine* followed more than twelve thousand people over thirty-two years and found that when one person gains weight, his close friends tend to gain weight too. Plato is spot on: "Like attracts like."

Playgrounds and Playmates

Early on, Alcoholics Anonymous discovered the same principle. At AA, your colleagues will regularly remind you: To overcome your addiction you will need to change your playmates and your playgrounds. If you are accustomed to hanging around with people who drink a lot, and spending time in places where alcohol flows in abundance, overcoming your addiction to alcohol will be challenging. To become healthy, you will need to change your patterns to be with healthy people in healthy settings. Like attracts like.

The same principle applies to your spiritual life. St. Paul put it this way: "Bad company ruins good morals" (1 Corinthians 15:33). If you are working to become the-best-version-of-yourself, surround yourself with people who are pursuing the same goal. If you want to become more generous, spend time with generous people. If you are seeking to get to the Place, go where other people are focused on that purpose too. Let the people around you inspire you, encourage you, and spur you on toward your goal.

It's true. We need a community to help us reach our goal. Faith is not an individual journey; it's a team sport. We need each other. We are on this journey together. And that is what a healthy community does. It makes you better.

If you need a community to become the-best-version-of-yourself, then so will your grandchild. Good news! God has already created that community for you. It's called the Church.

Research shows that young adults who grow up connected to a faith community are much more likely to remain in the faith as adults. More plainly, young adults who grow up active in a parish are more likely to be Catholics as adults and to be engaged in the Catholic faith as they mature.

God's Great Family

What's the number one image used in the New Testament to describe the Church? Family. In fact, the authors use that image more than two hundred times to capture who and what the Church is. We are family.

That's why you read so many verses like "Keep on loving each other as brothers and sisters" (Hebrews 13:1).

God has designed you to be a part of His family, the Church. And He has defined the Church as a community who loves like a big, healthy family—like brothers and sisters, eternally. We are God's forever family. One, holy, catholic, apostolic Church.

Think of everything your earthly family has in common. You share your name, your bloodline, your ancestors, your home, and you probably share lots of meals.

Now think about how much more we members of God's great family have in common as the Church. We share spiritual bonds and power that cannot be found anywhere else. Think about it. We share:

- the Holy Spirit (2 Corinthians 13:13)
- the divine nature of God (2 Peter 1:4)
- our material resources and possessions (Romans 15:27)
- a ministry with and to the saints (2 Corinthians 8:4)
- the sufferings of one another and of Jesus (Philippians 3:10)
- and best of all, we share the precious Body and Blood of Jesus Himself (1 Corinthians 10:16)

We share the very nature of God. Our shared meal is the Body and Blood of our Lord Jesus Christ. The sacraments offer regular invitations to experience holy moments, and the Eucharist is a holy moment beyond all else. You can only find that in your family, the Church.

This is no ordinary family. These deep spiritual family bonds create opportunities for us to experience holy moments unlike anything the world has to offer. Holy moments occur when we are aware that we are doing and being exactly who God wants us to be. We sense His presence around us and with us. After all, the Holy Spirit Himself is present when we gather as the Church.

Research shows that your grandchildren are more likely to embrace the faith if they have numerous holy moments along the way in which they experience the presence of God and a glimpse of the-best-version-of-themselves. Where are those holy moments most likely to occur? With God's family in the Church.

Research also proves that your grandchildren are more likely to be active Catholics if they have been connected to a parish throughout most or all of their formative years. Why would you not do all that you can to weave God's great family into their lives?

A community helps create belief. Like attracts like. The parish will help reinforce what you are doing to pass the torch. There, your grandchild will find more love, more personal coaching and mentors, help with formation in the faith, and healthy peers with the same deep desires to lift each other up, just like teammates do on a soccer field. *Keep on loving each other as brothers and sisters.*

Perhaps most important of all, the Church will be there even after you are gone. When your grandson is on his own to choose his path, the Church will still be there. You may not be, but the Church most certainly will.

When Charlie left for college, his entire family knew he was now on his own. His decisions were his and his alone. His grandparents had invested in Charlie's faith for many years, and now hoped he would find his way to a campus ministry where he would be surrounded by friends, and a parish where he would find a sense of belonging and place. But everyone also knew that it was now only in Charlie's control.

For the first few weeks, the family at home missed Charlie terribly. They wondered how things were going. Was he meeting and making good friends? Was he getting settled and putting down roots? Was his faith being nourished? And, of course, was he going to class? They communicated often, but it is hard to get an accurate reading merely through text messages and phone conversations.

About a month into his first semester, Charlie and his grandfather spoke on the phone. Grandpa asked him how things were going at school. Charlie said he loved it. Grandpa asked what was his favorite thing going on right now. And Charlie uttered the words no one would ever have imagined: "I love going to church. Right now, it is the only place that feels like home."

The *place* that feels like *home!* Charlie's exact words.

A sense of divine blessing rushed over Charlie's grandfather. Those words expressed his deepest hope and desire for his grandson as he set out on his own. Charlie had made the decision for himself: Jesus and His Church were his home. His family.

You Need the Church

We were made for each other.

This is partly because there is strength in numbers. Just as one coal struggles to hold a flame and heat on its own, one soul struggles to hold the flame of faith without the help of other souls surrounding it.

But we were made for each other also because we complete each other. We are all parts of the same story. I read years ago that each of us is like a single letter or punctuation mark. You may be a capital *S*, maybe your granddaughter is a lowercase *f*, and your grandson is a semicolon. God takes each of you and places you around the other people in the parish and the entire Church. He arranges all those markings into a beautiful story, perhaps a hymn like Psalm 23.

The Lord is my shepherd, I shall not want;
He makes me lie down in green pastures.

He leads me beside still waters;
He restores my soul.
He leads me in paths of righteousnes for His name's sake.
Even though I walk through the valley of the shadow of death,
I fear no evil;
for thou art with me;
thy rod and thy staff,
they comfort me.
Thou preparest a table before me
in the presence of my enemies;
thou anointest my head with oil,
my cup overflows.
Surely goodness and mercy shall follow me
all the days of my life;
and I shall dwell in the house of the Lord
forever.

On its own a single letter does not amount to much. On the other hand, when arranged as part of a majestic hymn to God, that single letter becomes indispensable and lovely. The poetry is incomplete without it. For example, remove the letter *s* from the psalm and it no longer comes together as art. In fact, it no longer even makes sense.

In the same way, your grandchild has a part to play in the genius of God. She will find her place among all the other letters, words, and punctuation marks. They in turn will elevate her to help her find her place in a beautiful piece of art.

This is God's dream for the Church, that we each find our place in His artistry. Because the Church's work is incomplete without every one of us. The Church is designed by God as the place for us to find our place.

On a mission trip to Nicaragua with the teens of my home parish, we worked with special needs children who had been abandoned by their families. Most of these children were severely developmentally challenged or disabled by the world's standards. But a group of faithful Catholics in Nicaragua has created a place—a home—for them.

Once a week, a local priest comes to celebrate Mass in the chapel with the kids at the Mustard Seeds community, with abandoned kids in the second-poorest country in the Western Hemisphere. These are kids who are poor, vulnerable, and desperate. Even when they grow into adults, they will always have a home in that portion of God's family on a little plot of land in Nicaragua.

This community serves kids like Juan, who was found on the streets years ago. He doesn't speak. No one knows anything about him or his family of origin. Juan has Down syndrome and is probably in his thirties, by our best guess. He's very gentle and will stay with the Mustard Seeds for as long as he lives.

After Mass each week, the kids form a procession around the chapel as the priest carries the host in a monstrance. The kids sing, shout, and dance around the chapel as they follow the priest and the sacrament. Leading the procession in the front is Juan, ringing a bell to the fullest with a huge smile on his face. He has found his place. And the joy overflows.

As I watched that procession parade in front of me, for a moment, I was not sure where we were. It was as if we were on the stairway to heaven; it was sheer joy. Each of those children, as well as the adults who serve them, has found his or her place in God's artistry. It's a place of total delight.

Finally, we were also made for each other because the Church is the healthiest and happiest place on earth. Just look at the science. Scientific journals are filled with studies demonstrating that active engagement in a parish or faith community leads to lower suicide rates, longer life spans, more attentive and faithful fathers, and deeper reported levels of satisfaction and meaning in life. We were made for each other and to find our place in God's family.

Who doesn't want that for their grandchild?

Recall the research from Columbia University that shows that the highest insulator against depression is the sharing of the faith by the child, the mother, and the grandmother. Nothing else helps decrease the chances of depression like that active shared faith. We walk this path together.

We all have our hurts and our pains. None of us are immune, even in the Church. The Church is not perfect. But only God's family is His chosen vessel for help and hope in the world. Only there are we inspired to love, teach, encourage, support, pray for, correct, heal, and honor one another, and to bear one another's burdens.

This is the next vital step in laying the foundation for happiness with God in your grandchild's life. Connecting with God's family will not only create those holy moments and a sense of belonging in your grandchild's life now, it will keep on doing that long after you are gone.

Pass the Torch

Now is the time to establish this engagement with God's family, together with your grandchild. The more engaged in the Church you are, the more engaged your grandchild will be. When you go to Mass, take your granddaughter with you. Invite your grandson to Adoration or confession at the parish with you. When there is an age-appropriate event at the parish for your grandson, offer to drive him and handle the logistics. When there is a children's choir concert, attend and applaud as your granddaughter sings. When the parish picnic and cookout begins, place your blanket on the ground and join in the activities alongside your grandson so that he feels enveloped by God's forever family.

If you live far away from your grandson, when the teens in his parish go on a mission trip, offer to go as a chaperone, pray each day for the teens, or help to fund the journey. If distance prevents you from attending Mass regularly with your granddaughter, send her a text each weekend. Share what you heard God saying to you at Mass and then ask her what God said to her that weekend. Or send her a picture of the liturgical decorations in your parish and ask her to respond with one from hers. Keep the regular conversation about parish life going.

In other words, when your grandchild expresses an interest in anything at the parish, let your first answer be yes. Then figure out how to make it happen, whether you live nearby or not. You are passing the torch to a new generation and weaving your grandchild into the genius and beauty of God's family, forever.

Nothing could be greater.

STEP SIX: CONNECT your grandchild **creatively** to a parish community.

———

Key Point
The Church will help you pass the torch, both now and forever.

Question to Consider
If every member of your parish participated just like you, what kind of parish would it become?

Action Step

Sponsor or volunteer to help with your grandchild's age group or in a multigenerational setting to weave him or her into God's family. Just be sure to go together. You will make all the difference.

If you live far away, consider timing your vacation to coincide with a time when your grandchild has something going on in his parish. That way, you can be present and celebrate that connection to the community. And your sacrifice of time and vacation will not go unnoticed or unappreciated by your grandchild.

Prayer

Lord, thank you for your Church. Amen.

One Helpful Tool

If your grandchild is young, enjoy together the free animated series for *Blessed*, Dynamic Catholic's first reconciliation and first Communion resource (dynamiccatholic.com/blessed). If you live far apart, all these videos are available online; you can watch them independently and then discuss by phone or text.

If your grandchild is an adolescent, enjoy together the free videos for *Decision Point*, Dynamic Catholic's confirmation program (dynamiccatholic.com/decisionpoint). Again, the videos are available online, so distance need not prevent you from sharing this with your grandchild.

10. STEP SEVEN: **INSPIRE** INTENTIONALLY

---

*It is Jesus who stirs in you the desire to do
something great with your lives . . .*
—St. John Paul II

I don't know what heaven looks like. But I have been to the Atlanta airport.

There's No Place like Home

My hometown, Atlanta, houses the busiest airport in the world. It's gargantuan, and it's awful. When your plane lands in Atlanta, you get off the plane, walk two hundred yards down a concourse, and then go down an escalator to get on a train. The train travels underneath the runways and eventually stops below the terminal. When you get off the train, you then step onto a massive escalator to take you up to street level to reach baggage claim and ground transportation.

I have never seen an escalator anywhere else that is remotely the size of this one at the Atlanta airport. It's probably four stories high. It goes up and up and up, nearly into the clouds. When you arrive at the top of that escalator, you enter a large common area where people stand waiting to welcome and receive arriving passengers.

That waiting area is more like a greeting area, really. This spot is the closest anyone who is waiting to meet your arrival in Atlanta can get to you without going through security. They stand at the top of that steep four-story escalator and wait for you to pop up on one of the three moving stairways.

In that waiting area stand greeters with signs, balloons, and eager faces full of anticipation. Chauffeurs and drivers wait with little signs that read BILL MITCHELL or THE FRANTZ PARTY. Children frantically anticipate Mom's appearance as she comes home from a long trip to Indiana. A young woman caresses her engagement ring as she awaits her fiancé, who is arriving home from a business trip to New York. College fraternity brothers bounce around anticipating the arrival of a friend coming to town for the weekend. A mother and father wait for their son to land, home from his deployment in Afghanistan. The USO volunteers lead cheers each time a soldier pops up at the top of the escalator.

Eyes sparkle with eagerness. "A special person is about to arrive, and we are here to welcome them!" The entire area percolates with energy as greeters wait and peer at the top of the escalator when each passenger pops into view.

"Will the next one be Mommy?"

"Is that our son?"

"Isn't she supposed to be here by now?"

I love to stand and watch these happy reunions. The waiting area just tingles with delight. Passengers arrive to squeals of joy, roars of laughter, streams of tears, bear hug embraces, and twirls in the arms of family.

I imagine heaven looks a lot like that. Each of us arrives into the presence of God, appearing on the horizon like travelers from a faraway land. We pop up one at a time at the top of a rising escalator. Our family members and heavenly greeting team stand waiting, tingling with delight and joy as they anticipate our arrival. One day, you and I are going to come up a very large escalator to the smiles, tears, and embraces of heaven's welcoming committee.

Greeters burst with heavenly joy when someone arrives from below. When you come up that escalator, you will hear wonderful words like, "Oh, we're so glad you're here. Welcome home. We have a place here just for you. Well done!"

That's what it will be like to be a part of the family of God.

Just in case God asks who I want to be there to welcome me, I've got my list ready. My own desired heavenly greeting team includes my grandmother, as well as Sts. Augustine, John Fisher, John Paul II, Teresa of Ávila, Gertrude the Great, and Teresa of Calcutta, and of course, Blessed Mary—all waiting to receive me as the newest arrival into the family of God once and for all.

Most of all, I hope Jesus Himself, arms outstretched, leads the event for each one of us, with a massive welcoming embrace and the words each of us hopes to hear: "Well done, good and faithful servant. Welcome home!"

Imagine the joy of arriving at the top of that escalator, to be met by that team.

Now imagine the greater joy of becoming a part of that welcoming team as you and Christ Jesus welcome your grandson or granddaughter by name into the presence of God. You have done your earthly job well. Your entire family celebrates an eternal reunion with Him in your new heavenly home.

You have passed the torch. You have helped your grandchild arrive at the Place. "Well done, good and faithful servant."

Crock-Pots, Not Microwaves

St. Paul compares our life journey to running a race. It's a marathon, not a sprint.

Getting to heaven takes a lifetime. Or, if you are a cook, the journey is more like a Crock-Pot than a microwave.

Helping your grandchild get to the Place is a long-distance journey. With your beautiful vocation as a grandparent, you have been given the opportunity to inspire your grandchild for a lifetime.

And you can inspire your grandchild in two key ways. First, while you are alive, by using the steps I have outlined for you in this book—praying, loving, and building habits—and by being there physically and spiritually in every way you can.

Second, God has given you a remarkable opportunity to keep inspiring your grandchild on toward the Place after your earthly life has ended. Check out these words from Scripture:

> Therefore since *we are surrounded by so great a cloud of witnesses,* let us also lay aside every weight and sin which clings so closely and let us run with perseverance the race that is set before us . . . (Hebrews 12:1, emphasis added)

When you cross the river from this lifetime, you become a part of a great cloud of witnesses—the gathering and cheering section of those who have gone before us; the souls who cheer and spur on those who come after us, helping them to run the race too.

In fact, St. John says your prayers surround the very throne of God. Like golden bowls of incense, your prayers are fragrant in the nostrils of God (see Revelation 5:8). Long after you have left this life, you will still be praying and encouraging your grandchild to finish the race, to get to the Place.

But before you leave this world, you have the opportunity to leave behind four precious gifts to inspire your grandchild for a lifetime.

Leave Four Gifts

Leave your grandchildren four gifts and you will help them finish the race you have begun together. These four gifts will propel them forward to that day when we will celebrate our family reunion with God in the kingdom once and for all.

1. *Leave mementos*

On my desk lies a Bible, a gift from my grandfather and grandmother. It's a visible reminder not only of their love for me but of a physical presence that stays with me and inspires me forward. I know they passed the torch to me then and are praying and cheering for me now to complete the race.

As Catholics we have lots of built-in opportunities to leave special mementos. The gift of a rosary at first Communion. A Bible at confirmation. A photo of you all together for a baptism. An album of memories from Christmas celebrations each year. A Miraculous Medal on a dog-tag or necklace chain. The gift of a ring for a wedding.

On top of that, you can provide special gifts that will stay with your grandchild always. A crucifix necklace as a birthday gift. Or the framed pictures of Jesus with children that hung in my daughters' bedrooms for years and that now hang in my grandsons' bedrooms.

We cherish, and even wear, special mementos so that memories stay with us. Your influence will transcend time as the past spills not only into the present but well into the future. Those mementos you leave with your grandchildren will continue to speak to them and inspire them long after you have gone.

2. Leave stories

Jesus spoke mostly in stories; He loved them. Because stories stick with us. We remember them. And we chew on them over and over again. Through stories, the past spills into the present and keeps shaping the future.

Stories bind families together. They are like the mortar that holds the bricks in place for the family home. Good stories define who our family is. Family stories remind us of what matters most. And those stories also remind us of the cast of characters who, albeit imperfectly, did their best to love us and show us the way.

There are good family stories of faith. Take, for example, the man who was asked where the faith in his family came from. "This is the way it came into my family of origin. Both of my parents were from families that were virtually without faith. My dad was the first one in his family to become involved in the Church, when he was converted to Catholicism. One time I said to my father, 'Dad, there is no one else in your family that is part of a community of faith. How did you start going to the Catholic Church?' He said, 'It was on the battlefields of Europe during World War II. I met a priest who was just one of us—plain, ordinary. Laid in the muddy foxholes with everyone else.'" That single event started the legacy. And the story keeps reminding that family, "This is who we are."

There are good family stories of failures or lessons discovered. Paul Haggis became the first screenwriter to win back-to-back Best Film Oscars. His grandfather became a janitor in a bowling alley in America after he left England because of a scandal no one knows the details of. He died when Paul was twelve or thirteen years old. Before he died, Paul's grandfather turned to him and said, "I've wasted my life. Don't waste yours." Those words still haunt him, but they also inspire and motivate him to live a life that matters. Stories keep speaking to us long after we first hear them.

Most of all, there are good family stories of love. My friend Chuck grew up in New York City. His grandparents emigrated from Italy to the United States. But a few years after landing here, Chuck's grandfather contracted tuberculosis, and the health authorities institutionalized him. He was no longer able to see or visit anyone outside the facility. His illness cut him off entirely from his wife, his children, and his entire family. That separation caused Chuck's grandfather enormous emotional pain, so much so that one night he snuck out of the asylum and desperately ran home. When the authorities discovered he was missing, they immediately came to the door of his home. They found Chuck's grandfather on the floor, hugging his children tightly. As the authorities took him away, the kids knew they would never see their father again. But they did know he loved them passionately. And every child needs to know that. The story still defines Chuck's family and reminds them of a grandfather's deep, deep love for the generations, the family, who would come after him.

Stories have power. They shape the present. And stories inspire the destinies of families.

Leave the gift of your stories. Stories about you, about your marriage, about your parents and grandparents. Stories about the Church, your faith, and great priests. Stories about how a saint changed your life. Populate your family with stories of greatness and love, and those stories will change the future.

3. *Leave memories*

Let your goal be to have created so many memories with your granddaughter that there is no way on earth she can think about life and big choices without thinking about your influence.

Your grandchild's inner world begins at a very early age. That means you get the opportunity to populate his inner world with experiences and conversations, stories about God and the saints, and images of places you have visited together. By doing this, you are creating memories. Some memories will pop into his mind often; others will lie beneath the surface, bubbling and shaping your grandchild for the rest of his life, even when he is not aware. The love you share now, the experiences you create together, and the holy moments you experience as grandparent and grandchild will last a lifetime. Play. Listen. Love. Create those memories well.

For actor Liev Schreiber, his grandfather made all the difference. When his parents divorced early on, Liev's grandfather Alex saved his money to help his daughter gain custody of Liev. From that point on, Alex essentially functioned as his dad. It was at his grandfather's house that Liev experienced Jewish seder meals and holy rabbis, moments that still infuse his life today—so much so that he would say every role he's ever played is an extension of his daydreaming about his grandfather. Powerful memories still live in his dreams.

In my case, I was in the second grade, Mrs. Blythe's class, the day my parents picked me up early from school. My brother, James, an eighth grader, was already in the car, and our family drove over the mountain from our town into another.

When we arrived, we parked in the driveway. My father got us together and led us up the walkway to the house. We walked in the door and saw the woman's familiar face, although it was missing the familiar smile. She walked down the hall, then came back and said, "He's ready."

My father took my brother and me by the hands and walked us down the hall, to the second door on the right and into the bedroom. He then turned and left, closing the door quietly behind him. There we were, James and I, looking across the room at the bed, on which lay an old man, formerly over six feet tall and near 180 pounds. Now, because of cancer, his body had withered down to 130 pounds or so. He was barely recognizable to us.

He asked us, "Are you ready?"

"Yes," we replied.

He told us, "Get a pencil and paper. Write this down."

We looked around the room until we each found a pencil and some scrap paper.

He asked us again, "Are you ready?"

"Yes."

He opened his lips and said, "Always remember who you are."

I remember. I wrote it down. In fact, I still carry that piece of paper in the Bible I use whenever I speak.

I still remember because those were the last words my grandfather ever said to me.

"Always remember who you are."

I wrote it down on a little slip of paper that day, and I carry that paper with me in my Bible. The memory shapes me every single day.

4. *Leave habits*

Most important of all, leave the gift of habits. After all, our lives change when our habits change.

At this point in the book, you have begun to use step five, Build Habits Boldly, to its fullest. You are helping to instill the habits that will lead your grandchild to greatness, the four life-changing habits that will help your grandchild's dreams become a reality—the four habits that bring happiness with God.

Pray. Study. Give. Evangelize.

Leave those habits as a gift in your grandchild's life and your grandchild will live well. Those habits will be the lasting residue of your own love and life with your family. They will serve like you, walking alongside your grandchild all the way to heaven.

Better still, your grandson will know you are cheering him on from that great cloud of witnesses. He will be able to sense it and draw strength from it each time he prays or gives. Your presence will be with him always.

Well Done

Do these things well. Leave these four gifts. Then live in the knowledge that you have passed the torch.

You'll be like Tim's grandmother. Tim suffers from Tourette's syndrome, a disorder characterized by physical and verbal tics, which went undiagnosed for the first ten years of his life.

In various interviews, he has said, "I didn't experience peace. But even though my life often seemed chaotic, I knew I could always count on at least one person to provide calm and stability: my grandmother. Nana's sense of peace was so powerful because it came from her faith in the Lord. Through her, God revealed His love for me as well. It wasn't long before I was following in her footsteps. I wanted the same kind of faith and peace she had, and that is exactly what God gave me."

Living with Tourette's is not an easy thing to do. "I just try to rely on faith. . . . I stumble, as many people do, but always in the belief that I'm loved and that I'm meaningful.

"Today, I am blessed to be living a dream. And yet, if it all went away tomorrow, I know I would still have peace. That probably sounds crazy to most people, but that's the kind of peace Christ gives. It is rooted in His love, and it surpasses all understanding."

Tim Howard has Tourette's syndrome and is a two-time World Cup goalie on his way to the Place. Why? Because his grandmother passed the torch.

What a blessing to know that you have lived well, and to live in the deepest hope of all. Your grandchild will have received the torch from you. You will have laid the foundation for a life filled with happiness with God. You will know that the fire was lit, by you.

Best of all, you will look forward to hearing those delightful words: "Well done, good and faithful servant."

Indeed, well done.

STEP SEVEN: INSPIRE intentionally your grandchild's entire life by leaving behind four special gifts.

=====

Key Point

The journey is eternal. Leave behind four special gifts, and then keep on cheering. The best is yet to come.

Question to Consider

"My wishes for my grandchild are . . ."

Action Step

Write a letter to be opened at a special time later in your grandchild's life (e.g., on his twenty-first birthday, on her wedding day, after the birth or baptism of your first great-grandchild).

Prayer

Lord, help me pass the torch. Amen.

One Helpful Tool

Share an important thought with your grandchild. Ask him or her to write it on a piece of paper as a special message to keep as inspiration." Share an important thought with your grandchild. Ask him or her to write it on a piece of paper as a special message to keep as inspiration."

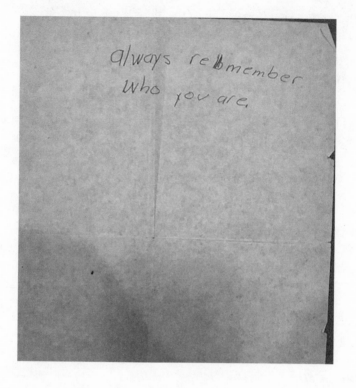

EPILOGUE

In every life and in every family, there are a precious few moments when all good things possible can be claimed. Moments when key decisions are made. Moments when opportunities are either seized or lost. There are critical choices that, when looked back upon at the end of your life, will be seen to have been pivotal. They are choices that determined who you became and, just as important, what became of your family and your grandchildren. Those key moments are unfolding in your life right now as you are reading this very page.

Some moments occur in the blink of an eye. Others accumulate a little at a time as hours turn into days, days into weeks, and weeks into years. It would be a great gift to know what to choose, what to do, and how to do it at that critical time.

With this book, my goal was to create something that had the potential to become one of those moments, one of those opportunities to help you know what you need to know, when you need to know it. My hope was to plant the seed to help you see the key steps that lead grandchildren to happy lives and greatness. And to help you see the key role you play in it as a grandparent, when you are paying attention and even when you are not. God has given you this special vocation.

You now hold a key chain with the master keys of grandparenting, seven steps to help you achieve your dream, whether that's to pass the torch, to light the fire, or simply to help your grandchild lead a happy life. These are the keys you need regardless of the structure, geography, and style of your family. These steps lead us all to God, the Place.

Knowing your critical role and then taking these seven specific steps to greatness will help you lead your grandchild into the future you dream and hope for. You have been given the plan. I now invite you to have the courage and the passion to attain it.

All this preparation for leading your family should be at the core of your mission in this life. As you create the rhythm of your family, treat it with care and devotion. This is your vocation. God is nudging you forward. The time for action, the time for leadership, is now.

That is why I wrote this book. There is a great tug-of-war going on as the culture seeks to overwhelm your grandchild. As a grandparent, you must never give up. You must be willing to be the anchor and strength in your family. Your strong leadership and faith will be your family's compass for their journey.

To this day, decades since he passed from this life, I can still hear my grandfather's voice telling me, "Always remember who you are." You can be that compass for your own family. I know you can. And it is not too late. Step up. Make the plans. Lead the way.

My own dream? I hope to be like Rebecca's grandmother. When Rebecca was in third grade, the teacher gave the class an assignment: Write three sentences about your hero.

With that assignment in hand, Rebecca wrote these words:

Who Is a Hero to You?

My hero is my grandma because she is very kind, nice, helpful, generous, and loving. She loves God a lot.

She is a good hero.

Rebecca is a grown woman now, with kids of her own, but she continues to hang on to that third-grade assignment, keeping the paper in a special place to preserve it. Rebecca wants to remember, to be inspired by her grandmother. Her grandmother showed her the way.

May you and I live long, full lives filled with kindness, generosity, and love. And most of all, may our grandchildren know that we love God, a lot.

He established a testimony in Jacob
and appointed a law in Israel,
which he commanded our fathers
to teach to their children;
that the next generation would know them,
the children yet unborn,
and arise and tell them to their children,
so that they should set their hope in God,
and not forget the works of God,
but keep his commandments.
(Psalm 78:5–7)